Mother Goose Rhymes for the Night

Kimberly K. Faurot

Illustrated by Steve Cox

Musical Notations by Sara L. Waters

Fort Atkinson, Wisconsin
www.upstartbooks.com

Acknowledgments
Saroj Ghoting, Early Literacy Consultant

Special thanks to the following individuals and institutions:
Brad Kruse
Steve Cox
Sara L. Waters
Kristi McNellis
Lyle and JoAnne Faurot
Cathy Norris and the Children's Department staff, past and present,
of the Hedberg Public Library, Janesville, WI
Carmel Clay Public Library Children's Department, Carmel, IN
Dr. Shirley Fitzgibbons
Jim Peitzman
Ann Denton
St. Paul Public Library, St. Paul, MN
University of Minnesota Libraries

All Highsmith/Upstart staff who worked on this project, including:
Matt Mulder, Publisher
Michelle McCardell, Managing Editor
Heidi Green, Art Director
Joann Lueck, Graphic Designer
Matt Napier, Production Designer
Sandy Harris, Product Development Manager

Published by UpstartBooks
W5527 State Road 106
P.O. Box 800
Fort Atkinson, Wisconsin 53538-0800
1-800-448-4887

Text © Kimberly K. Faurot, 2006
Illustrations © Steve Cox, 2006

The paper used in this publication meets the minimum requirements of American National Standard for Information Science—Permanence of Paper for Printed Library Material. ANSI/NISO Z39.48-1992.

All rights reserved. Printed in the United States of America.
The purchase of this book entitles the individual librarian or teacher to reproduce copies for use in the library or classroom. The reproduction of any part for an entire school system or for commercial use is strictly prohibited. No form of this work may be reproduced or transmitted or recorded without written permission from the publisher.

Contents

Introduction 5
- Before You Begin 5
- Why Nursery Rhymes? 5
- Early Literacy 5
- For All Ages 6
- How to Use this Book 6
- References: Nursery Rhymes and Early Literacy 11

Diddle Diddle Dumpling 13
- Rhyme 13
- Variants 13
- History 13
- Preparing and Using the Mother Goose Rhyme Time Pieces 13
- Storytime 13
- Early Literacy Activities 14
- Take-home "Diddle Diddle Dumpling" 16
- Additional Extension Ideas 16
- Musical Notation 18
- Take-home Reproducible 19

Hey Diddle Diddle 21
- Rhyme 21
- Variants 21
- History 21
- Preparing and Using the Mother Goose Rhyme Time Pieces 21
- Storytime 22
- Early Literacy Activities 22
- Take-home "Hey Diddle Diddle" 25
- Additional Extension Ideas 25
- Musical Notation 27
- Take-home Reproducible 28

Jack Be Nimble 31
- Rhyme 31
- Variants 31
- History 31
- Preparing and Using the Mother Goose Rhyme Time Pieces 31
- Storytime 32
- Early Literacy Activities 32
- Take-home "Jack Be Nimble" 34
- Additional Extension Ideas 34
- Musical Notation 36
- Take-home Reproducible 37

Little Boy Blue 39
- Rhyme 39
- Variants 39
- History 39
- Preparing and Using the Mother Goose Rhyme Time Pieces 39
- Storytime 40
- Early Literacy Activities 40
- Take-home "Little Boy Blue" 43
- Additional Extension Ideas 43
- Musical Notation 44
- Take-home Reproducible 54

The Man in the Moon 49
- Rhyme 49
- Variants 49
- History 49

Preparing and Using the Mother Goose Rhyme Time Pieces 49

Storytime 50

Early Literacy Activities 50

Take-home "The Man in the Moon" 52

Additional Extension Ideas 53

Musical Notation 55

Take-home Reproducible 56

There Was an Old Woman Tossed Up in a Basket 57

Rhyme 57

Variants 57

History 57

Preparing and Using the Mother Goose Rhyme Time Pieces 58

Storytime 58

Early Literacy Activities 59

Take-home "There Was an Old Woman Tossed Up in a Basket" 61

Additional Extension Ideas 61

Musical Notation 63

Take-home Reproducible 64

Bibliographies and Resources 67

Mother Goose Collections to Share and Recommend 67

History of Nursery Rhymes 67

Mother Goose Crafts 68

Mother Goose Songbooks 68

Sound Recordings 68

Spanish Language Resources 69

Where to Buy Sound Recordings 69

Where to Buy Alphabet Letters 70

Storybook and Sound Recording Titles Listed in *Mother Goose Rhyme Time: Night* 70

Mother Goose and Early Literacy Programming Books, Articles, and Video/DVDs 70

Mother Goose Programming and Early Literacy Web Connections 71

Introduction

Each Mother Goose Rhyme Time book is designed as a companion to a large size Mother Goose poster and character set. The books enhance the characters' possibilities by providing brief histories of each rhyme, simple musical notations so the rhymes may be played and sung, and suggestions for successfully incorporating the rhymes into library storytimes or classroom lessons.

Before You Begin

Punch out, laminate, and assemble the character cutouts as directed on the punch-out pages. Create an organized storage system so each poster and its accompanying pieces are easily accessible and safe from damage.

Why Nursery Rhymes?

Researchers have determined that young children who know nursery rhymes have a distinct advantage over those who do not as they embark upon the journey toward literacy (Bryant, Bradley, MacLean, and Crossland 426).

Nursery rhymes specifically foster and enhance:

- Acquisition of new vocabulary and concepts
- Oral language abilities, including the internalization of characteristic speech rhythms and intonation patterns
- Phonological awareness/sensitivity, the ability to recognize that spoken words consist of sound segments
- Sensitivity to and ability to detect rhyme and alliteration

Targeted nursery rhyme activities may additionally be used to help develop memorization skills, narrative skills and sequencing, print motivation, print awareness and tracking, and letter knowledge.

The linguistic routines inherent in nursery rhymes provide opportunities for children to hear sound similarities and differences, consequently developing and enhancing their phonological skills (MacLean, Bryant, and Bradley 277). In turn, phonological awareness is a key factor in eventual mastery of reading and spelling. This awareness of the smaller sounds in words does not develop automatically, in contrast to speech perception abilities, which are typically natural and spontaneous (National Research Council 51–57). Encouraging these phonological skills through introduction to rhyme and alliteration helps establish a foundation for effective decoding, and ultimately is a critical skill for fluent reading later on.

Early Literacy

Nursery rhymes are one of the building blocks of early literacy, a perspective that emphasizes skill development through young children's positive interactions with books and with caregivers, and regular exposure to literacy-rich environments and experiences. Early literacy does not mean teaching actual reading earlier, but laying a firm foundation for reading later on (Zero to Three). As MacLean, Bryant, and Bradley note, "... children acquire phonological awareness a long time before learning to read, through experiences which at the time have nothing to do with reading" (278). Activities such as chewing on and handling books, looking at and pointing to storybook pictures, saying rhymes and singing songs, rudimentary recognition of and interest in letters of the alphabet, and scribbling all help establish a child's preliminary foundation of knowledge about reading and writing long before he or she is developmentally ready to actually read or write. Just as a baby's babbling is a precursor to formal speech, these and other early literacy behaviors are precursors to reading (Project ECLIPSE).

For All Ages

Nursery rhymes are ideal components of programs for very young children, who respond naturally to the verses' engaging meter. The rhymes' brevity makes them well suited to short attention spans, and their bounceable, jumpable, clappable rhythms make them helpful tools in engaging active young listeners.

Despite this natural affinity, many children are not introduced to nursery rhymes as infants or preschoolers, and consequently require formal exposure upon reaching school. As children grow, nursery rhymes can play a shifting yet vital role in their literacy development. Incorporating rhymes into storytimes and activities for older children can establish confidence in "reading" a rhyme that is already comfortable and known; enhance phonological awareness and subsequently reading abilities; and provide a springboard for lessons in such diverse subjects as math, punctuation, creative writing, and history. Comparing the illustrations from various versions of Mother Goose can develop visual literacy, and research techniques may be taught through investigating the rhymes' possible origins. Older children can reminisce about the wording of rhymes that they remember from their own early years, and then compare those versions to the many different adaptations available.

Nursery rhymes are similarly effective in the elementary ESL/ELL (English as a Second Language/English Language Learners) classroom, supplying interesting characters, opportunities for vocabulary development, and plenty of action. The rhymes' natural rhythms help students develop an understanding of English speech cadences and intonation, as they do with very young children just beginning to utilize spoken language. Since most cultures have their own traditional play rhymes and songs, students can share and teach these in their native language to classmates and teachers. Cultural rhymes, games, and songs can also provide an ideal venue for parent/caregiver involvement with a child's class, and for affirming the vital importance of each student's cultural identity. Assignments may include children learning traditional rhymes at home to subsequently share in school or as part of a special presentation for family members. Parents or caregivers can be invited to attend the class as visiting instructors to teach rhymes and songs from their own childhoods, encouraging appreciation for and recognition of their family's history.

In addition to the rhythms and phonological connections that nursery rhymes help promote, educators recognize that children must be familiar with the rhymes' content and meaning to understand many cultural allusions and references throughout their lives.

How to Use this Book

Utilize the sections of Mother Goose Rhyme Time that work best for you and your storytime group or classroom. Experiment with new ideas and techniques. Practice ahead of time so you feel comfortable with the material and can focus on the audience rather than on trying to remember how you intended to share the rhyme. Consider introducing "Mother Goose Rhyme Time" each week with a Mother Goose puppet or special song to signal what will happen next. For example:

> (Tune: "The Farmer in the Dell")
> It's time for Mother Goose
> I've heard she's on the loose!
> She'll bring a rhyme for storytime,
> It's time for Mother Goose!

Each chapter includes the following sections:

Rhyme

A standard version of the nursery rhyme, which matches the poster included in the companion set.

Variants

Alternate wording or versions of the rhyme that are different from the version in this book.

History

A brief historical note about the rhyme's possible origins. Occasionally sharing bits of background information can add to the rhyme's charm and entertainment value for parents and

caregivers as they find themselves inevitably reading it repeatedly with their child! The references may also be used as a familiar and engaging entry to older students' history lessons.

Musical Notation

Simple, storytime-tested melodies for each rhyme, with autoharp/guitar chords. Tunes reflect standard melodies if any are known, and offer straightforward new adaptations for rhymes with obscure historical tunes.

Preparing and Using the Mother Goose Rhyme Time Pieces

A list of the rhyme pieces and the poster are needed for presenting each rhyme, with preliminary preparation and presentation suggestions. For example, before sharing the rhyme, place the poster on an easel so the audience can see it clearly. For some rhymes, pieces may be stacked in reverse order of appearance and hidden out of sight before the audience arrives. Rhyme pieces may be held in the presenter's hands, glued or taped securely to a paint stirrer and held aloft, or affixed to a large Velcro or magnet board. If you wish to incorporate motions or use a musical instrument for accompaniment, point to each piece on the board in turn as you lead the group in the actions or play and sing the song.

Storytime

Ideas for sharing the nursery rhyme as a song or chant, with suggestions for various ways to repeat it. Sing or say the rhyme quickly and slowly, loudly and quietly, while bouncing, patting your lap, or clapping to keep a rhythm. Add movements and animal noises or snoring as desired, mimicking the action in the rhyme. Encourage the children's caregivers to adapt movements or make up new ones as appropriate for their child. Possible motions for babies and older children are included. Share one rhyme several times during a single storytime, and repeat the same rhyme over several storytimes.

Early Literacy Activities

These activities follow the seven focus areas recommended in Every Child Ready to Read @ Your Library, an early literacy partnership project between the Public Library Association and the Association for Library Service to Children, divisions of the American Library Association, and the National Institute of Child Health and Human Development (NICHD) of the National Institutes of Health (see www.pla.org/earlyliteracy.htm). A clear overview of these focus areas as well as innovative activity suggestions are included in *Early Literacy Storytimes @ Your Library* by Saroj Nadkarni Ghoting and Pamela Martin-Diaz (American Library Assn., 2006).

Consider integrating several (not all) of the Early Literacy Activities or techniques suggested below as you share the nursery rhyme. All activities should be approached in a fun and playful manner, encouraging curiosity and allowing for children's individual differences. Avoid any tendencies toward drill or rote memorization (Yopp 702). **Note:** Be aware of children's developmental stages and focus on the activities that are appropriate to the ages and stages of your group. The suggestions provided are intended to give you a variety of ideas to work with over time. You will not incorporate all of the techniques into any one rhyme, or even all into one storytime. Try different activities to highlight a different skill during each storytime.

Print Motivation

- Encourage interest in and excitement about reading and books. Say the words rhythmically and with enthusiasm.

- Create voices for the characters, and change your tone and facial expression as appropriate to the context to convey your enjoyment of the rhyme.

- Repeat the rhyme several times together with the children, encouraging their own enjoyment and internalization of its lively rhythms.

Language and Vocabulary

- Introduce and explain new words or new meanings to familiar words. Use the rhyme pieces to illustrate, pointing to the pictures of the words you are saying or the events you are describing.

- Talk or sing about the illustrations: "I see a haystack." "I see a cow." Pause for the children to name the object to which you are pointing: "I see a _____." Expand on descriptive features of the illustrations to build vocabulary and encourage the children's awareness of and attention to details. For example: "I see a boy. A boy wearing a blue hat and blue clothes."

Phonological Awareness

- Play with rhymes, practice breaking words apart and putting them back together, and listen for beginning sounds and alliteration. Play with the words, objects, and names in the rhyme and change them (see each chapter for examples). Use puppets or props to dramatize the alternate word choices.

- Explain that rhyming words sound the same at the end, and give examples. Try pausing just before the end of a rhyming pair and encourage the children to supply the rhyming word with the support of visual clues or context, or simply through the sounds suggested by the rhyme.

- Play an "oddity task" game. For example, which word does not rhyme? Horn, sheep, corn. *(Answer: sheep.)* Which word sounds different at the beginning? Diddle, fiddle, dog. *(Answer: fiddle.)* Which word sounds different at the end? Cat, hat, dog. *(Answer: dog.)*

- Blend word parts in a variety of ways.

    <u>Syllables:</u> dump ... ling. What's the word? *(Dumpling.)*

    <u>Onset sound:</u> /d/ ... og. What's the word? *(Dog.)* What other words start with /d/? (Note that the symbol / / signifies the sound of the letter.)

    <u>Phoneme by phoneme (for older children, in primary grades):</u> /m/-/oo/-/n/. What's the word? *(Moon.)*

- Practice segmenting or "stretching" the nursery rhyme words (for older children, in primary grades). Show the children a rubber band and stretch it out and in. As you stretch the rubber band out longer, you can see all of its parts more clearly. Explain that you can also stretch words, so that you can hear each individual sound (phoneme) in the word. Stretch the word "on": /o/-/n/. Sometimes one phoneme is represented by more than one letter, such as in the name "John": /J/-/oh/-/n/. "John" contains three phonemes. Stretch other nursery rhyme words.

- Clap words: Clap once for each word in the rhyme, following the poster. Introduce variety by stomping feet or jumping once for each word.

- Clap syllables: Slightly older children can learn to clap once for each syllable in the rhyme. Practice with one word at a time as the children begin to understand the concept. For example: Did-dle (2 claps); Did-dle (2 claps); Dump-ling (2 claps); my (1 clap); son (1 clap); John (1 clap). Introduce variety by stomping feet or jumping to the syllables.

- Sing the nursery rhyme to its familiar tune. Follow the musical notations and autoharp/guitar chords provided if desired.

Print Awareness

- Help the children notice print, know how to handle books, and follow the written word on a page. Point to the poster included in the companion kit and say: "Our nursery rhyme is written right up here. I'll read it aloud, and then we'll say it again together." Follow the text of the rhyme with your finger as you read the poster, from left to right to reinforce print directionality as well as the concept that print stands for spoken language.

- Occasionally turn the poster upside down or sideways and see if the children detect the problem.

Narrative Skills

- Practice retelling stories or events with the children, sequencing the order in which events happened, and adding descriptions. Talk and ask open-ended questions about

the rhyme and the objects and characters in it, and allow the children to ask questions. Avoid asking yes/no questions unless there is a specific purpose in doing so. Qualify questions by including the phrase, "do you think," such as in "Why do you think …?" or "What do you think …?" This type of question does not have a "right" answer that children are afraid they will get wrong. Talk about ways in which we may have experiences or feelings that are similar to those of the nursery rhyme characters. For example, how do you think Little Boy Blue will feel when he wakes up and finds that the sheep are in the meadow and the cows are eating the corn?

- If you have a small enough group and adequate time, act out the rhyme with creative dramatics. Make sure each child gets to play all of the roles if possible, and to choose who or what they want to be.

- Consider incorporating craft activities into the program as a springboard for the children to retell rhymes and stories. (See "Take-home Rhyme Pieces" and "Additional Extension Ideas" in each chapter.)

- As the children's repertoire of nursery rhyme friends grows, ask "Who am I?" nursery rhyme riddles. For example: "I blow my horn to call the sheep and the cows. I fell asleep under a haystack. Who am I?" *(Answer: Little Boy Blue.)*

Letter Knowledge

- Help the children learn to recognize and identify letters; to know that they have different names and sounds; and to understand that the same letter can look different. Begin with letter sounds that young children can articulate easily, and introduce the sounds in the general order they develop in children's speech. (See www.pla.org/ala/pla/plaissues/earlylit/workshopsparent/lettersounds.pdf.)

Choose word examples that correspond to the letter sounds. For example, "S is for Sock." Avoid word examples such as "S is for Sheep," which begins with the "sh" sound rather than a hard "s."

Introduce this group of letters first, one at a time, though not necessarily in this order:

B, M, D, T, W, P, N, Y, H

Introduce this group of letters next:

S, F, G, V, Z, K, C

Introduce this group of letters last:

L, R, J

Parent/Caregiver Connection

- Reinforce the parent/caregiver's key role in their child's early literacy development through comfortable, relaxed times together with songs, rhymes, and books.

- Encourage parents/caregivers to participate during storytime and to incorporate nursery rhymes at home during play and reading times. Select one of the early literacy activities that you share together during storytime, and briefly explain how the activity supports children's early literacy development. Suggest repeating the activity at home. Try different activities to highlight different skills during each storytime.

- Share information about Dialogic, or "Hear and Say" Reading (see Resources). Encourage parents and caregivers to individually discuss the day's rhyme, its characters, and events in an open-ended way with their children, following the child's interest while affirming and expanding upon their answers. Build on the things that catch the child's interest. This type of positive, interactive discussion around familiar rhymes and books helps improve early language development, communication, and parent/child relationships.

- Share brief facts about the direct benefits of reading to children and of playing word games with them.

- Model enthusiastic reading behaviors and interactions, emphasizing fun and enjoyment as the goals.

Take-home Rhyme Pieces

- Distribute take-home card stock illustrations of the day's nursery rhyme (included in each rhyme chapter), and either color and assemble them at the end of storytime or encourage the families to do so at home. Make a sample of the take-home version, and demonstrate singing or saying the rhyme using the small-size piece(s). (Families may affix sticky-back magnet material to pieces for playtime use on a magnetic surface such as a cookie sheet or the refrigerator if desired. Be aware of choking hazard considerations for younger children.)

Additional Extension Ideas

- Make companion crafts for the day's nursery rhyme, providing materials for both children and adults, or share storybooks extending the rhyme's theme, content, or concepts.

- Display nursery rhyme and children's poetry books and make them available for your audience to borrow and share at home. Emphasize that the books don't need to be read from cover to cover. Encourage children and their caregivers to take turns selecting poems and rhymes as they read, and to talk about details of illustrations that accompany the text. Show pictures from several different nursery rhyme books that illustrate the day's nursery rhyme, and repeat the rhyme together with each new illustration. Some classic and favorite Mother Goose books are listed in the bibliography.

- Build a nursery rhyme village, make a giant map of Mother Goose Town, orchestrate a Mother Goose Musical performance, or celebrate International Mother Goose Day (May 1).

- Let your creativity run wild, and have fun!

The ideas detailed in this volume, together with the nursery rhyme poster and character set from the companion kit, provide tools and techniques to help you successfully weave nursery rhymes and related activities into the fabric of your storytimes and curriculum. I hope that these methods will help you gain confidence and facility in sharing nursery rhymes, and also provide you with a deeper understanding of the enduring benefits afforded by actively sharing this rich tradition with your children, their families, and caregivers.

References

Nursery Rhymes and Early Literacy

Adams, Marilyn Jager. *Beginning to Read: Thinking and Learning About Print.* MIT Press, 1990.

Blevins, Wiley. *Phonemic Awareness Activities for Early Reading Success: Easy, Playful Activities That Prepare Children for Phonics Instruction.* Scholastic Professional Books, 1997.

Bryant, P. E., and L. Bradley, M. MacLean, J. Crossland. "Nursery Rhymes, Phonological Skills and Reading." *Journal of Child Language,* 16.2 (1989): 407–428.

Bryant, P. E., M. MacLean, L. L. Bradley, and J. Crossland. (1990). "Rhyme and Alliteration, Phoneme Detection, and Learning to Read." *Developmental Psychology,* 26.3 (1990): 429–438.

Fox, Mem. *Reading Magic: Why Reading Aloud to Our Children Will Change their Lives Forever.* Harcourt, 2001.

Geller, Linda Gibson. "Children's Rhymes and Literacy Learning: Making Connections." *Language Arts,* 60.2 (1983): 184–193.

Ghoting, Saroj Nadkarni, and Pamela Martin-Diaz. *Early Literacy Storytimes @ Your Library: Partnering with Caregivers for Success.* American Library Assn., 2006.

Hempenstall, Kerry. "The Role of Phonemic Awareness in Beginning Reading: A Review." *Behaviour Change,* 14 (1997): 201–214.

The International Reading Association and the National Association for the Education of Young Children. *Learning to Read and Write: Developmentally Appropriate Practices for Young Children.* www.naeyc.org/about/positions/pdf/PSREAD98.PDF. 1998.

Kirtley, Clare, Peter Bryant, Morag MacLean, and Lynette Bradley. "Rhyme, Rime, and the Onset of Reading." *Journal of Experimental Child Psychology,* 48 (1989): 224–245.

MacLean, Morag, Peter Bryant, and Lynette Bradley. "Rhymes, Nursery Rhymes, and Reading in Early Childhood." *Merrill-Palmer Quarterly,* 33.3 (1987): 255–281.

Morrow, Lesley Mandel. *Getting Ready to Read with Mother Goose.* Sadlier-Oxford, 2001.

Morrow, Lesley Mandel. *Literacy Development in the Early Years: Helping Children Read and Write.* 4th ed. Allyn & Bacon, 2001.

National Research Council. Catherine Snow, M. Susan Burns, and Peg Griffin, eds. *Preventing Reading Difficulties in Young Children.* National Academy Press, 1998.

Project ECLIPSE. "Mother Goose: A Scholarly Exploration." 31 Dec. 2005. www.eclipse.rutgers.edu/goose/literacy/.

Sadlier-Oxford. "Nursery Rhymes and Phonemic Awareness." Professional Development Series, Volume 3. Sadlier-Oxford, 2000.

Yopp, Hallie Kay. "Developing Phonemic Awareness in Young Children." *The Reading Teacher,* 45.9 (1992): 696–703.

Zero to Three. "Brain Wonders: Early Literacy." 31 Dec. 2005. www.zerotothree.org/brainwonders/EarlyLiteracy.html.

Diddle Diddle Dumpling

> Diddle diddle dumpling, my son John,
>
> Went to bed with his stockings on;
>
> One shoe off, and one shoe on,
>
> Diddle diddle dumpling, my son John.

Variants

Alternate versions of this rhyme begin with "Deedle, deedle, dumpling," and some list "trousers" or "breeches" instead of "stockings."

Also:

> My son John
> He went to bed with his breeches on.
> One shoe off and one shoe on,
> These were the deeds of my son John.

History

"Diddle, diddle, diddle Dumpling" was the street cry of the hot-dumpling sellers, likely the genesis of the rhyme's initial refrain. Further origins are unknown, although the rhyme was documented as early as 1797.

Musical Notation

See musical notation on page 18.

Preparing and Using the Mother Goose Rhyme Time Pieces

"Diddle Diddle Dumpling" pieces:

- Boy in bed wearing stockings, one shoe off and one shoe on
- "Diddle Diddle Dumpling" poster

Before sharing the rhyme, place the poster on an easel so the audience can see it clearly. Hold the slumbering John in one hand as you say the rhyme. With the other hand, hold up one finger and point to the foot with its shoe off, then hold up one finger again and point to the foot still wearing its shoe.

If you wish to incorporate motions or use a musical instrument for accompaniment, affix John to a Velcro or magnet board and point to him as you lead the group in the actions or play and sing the song.

Utilize the sections of Mother Goose Rhyme Time that work best for you and your storytime group or classroom. Experiment with new ideas and techniques. Practice ahead of time so you feel comfortable with the material and can focus on the audience rather than on trying to remember how you intended to share the rhyme.

Storytime

Share "Diddle Diddle Dumpling" as a song or as a chant; rocking back and forth, bouncing, patting your lap, or clapping to keep a rhythm. Sing or say the rhyme quickly and slowly, loudly and quietly. Incorporate movements and snoring as desired. Many different motions and actions are possible. Here are a few options:

Babies *(Sitting on caregivers' laps)*

Diddle diddle dumpling, my son John,
(Bicycle baby's legs.)
Went to bed with his stockings on;
One shoe off, and one shoe on,
(Pat each foot.)
Diddle diddle dumpling, my son John.
(Bicycle baby's legs.)

Older Children *(Standing or sitting)*

Diddle diddle dumpling, my son John,
(Clap hands rhythmically.)
Went to bed with his stockings on;
(Rest head on hands, then touch ankles.)
One shoe off, and one shoe on,
(Hold up one foot, then the other foot.)
Diddle diddle dumpling, my son John.
(Clap hands rhythmically.)

Early Literacy Activities

Consider integrating one or several of the activities or techniques suggested below as you share the nursery rhyme. All activities should be approached in a fun and playful manner, encouraging curiosity and allowing for children's individual differences. **Note:** Be aware of children's developmental stages and focus on the activities that are appropriate for the ages and stages of your group. The suggestions provided are intended to give you a variety of ideas to work with over time. You will not incorporate all of the techniques at once. Share one rhyme several times during a single storytime, and repeat the same rhyme over several storytimes. Try different activities to highlight a different skill during each storytime.

Print Motivation *(Encourage interest in and excitement about reading and books.)*

- Say the words rhythmically and with enthusiasm, conveying your enjoyment of the rhyme.

- Repeat the rhyme several times together with the children, encouraging their own enjoyment and internalization of its lively rhythms.

Language and Vocabulary *(Introduce and explain new words or new meanings to familiar words.)*

- Use the rhyme pieces to illustrate and help explain language and vocabulary. Say: "This boy's name is John *(point to John)*. He went to bed with his stockings on! His stockings are his socks *(point to John's stockings)*. He had one shoe off *(point to the shoe that is off)* and one shoe on his foot *(point to the shoe that is on)*."

- Talk or sing about the illustrations: "I see a shoe." "I see a bed." Pause for the children to name the object to which you are pointing: "I see a _____." Expand on descriptive features of the illustrations to build vocabulary and encourage the children's awareness of and attention to details: "I see a boy. A boy holding a brown teddy bear."

Phonological Awareness *(Play with rhymes, practice breaking words apart and putting them back together, and listen for beginning sounds and alliteration.)*

- Play with the words, objects, and names in the rhyme and change them. Use puppets or props to dramatize. For example:

Diddle diddle dumpling, my little cat,
Went to bed with an old pink hat;
A plate of milk, and a little toy bat,
Diddle diddle dumpling, my little cat.

- Explain that rhyming words sound the same at the end. "Cat" and "hat" and "bat" all rhyme. Try pausing just before the end of a rhyming pair and encourage the children to supply the rhyming word (such as "hat" and "bat" above) with the support of visual clues or context, or simply through the sounds suggested by the rhyme.

Diddle diddle dumpling, my girl Jill,
Came back home from climbing the hill;
Left her socks on the windowsill,
Diddle diddle dumpling, my girl Jill.

- Blend word parts in a variety of ways.

  <u>Syllables</u>: dump … ling. What's the word? *(Dumpling.)*

Onset sound: /b/ ... ed. What's the word? *(Bed.)* What other words start with /b/?

Phoneme by phoneme (for older children, in primary grades): /o/-/n/. What's the word? *(On.)*

- Practice segmenting or "stretching" the nursery rhyme words (for older children, in primary grades). Show the children a rubber band and stretch it out and in. As you stretch the rubber band out longer, you can see all of its parts more clearly. Explain that you can also stretch words, so that you can hear each individual sound (phoneme) in the word. Stretch the word "on": /o/-/n/. Sometimes one phoneme is represented by more than one letter, such as in the name "John": /J/-/oh/-/n/. "John" contains three phonemes. Stretch other nursery rhyme words.

- Clap words: Clap once for each word in the rhyme, following the poster. Introduce variety by stomping feet or jumping once for each word.

- Clap syllables: Older children can learn to clap once for each syllable in the rhyme. Practice with one word at a time as the children begin to understand the concept. For example: Did-dle (2 claps); did-dle (2 claps); dump-ling (2 claps); my (1 clap); son (1 clap); John (1 clap). Introduce variety by stomping feet or jumping to the syllables.

Print Awareness *(Notice print and know how to handle books and follow the written word on a page.)*

- Point to the "Diddle Diddle Dumpling" poster. Say: "Our nursery rhyme is written right up here. I'll read it aloud, and then we'll say it again together." Follow the text of the rhyme with your finger as you read the poster, from left to right.

- Occasionally turn the poster upside down or sideways and see if the children detect the problem.

Narrative Skills *(Practice retelling stories or events, sequencing the order in which events happened, and adding descriptions.)*

- Talk and ask two or three open-ended questions about the rhyme and the objects and characters in it, and allow the children to ask questions. Avoid asking yes/no questions unless there is a specific purpose in doing so. Qualify questions by including the phrase "do you think," as in "Why do you think ...?" or "What do you think ...?" This type of question does not have a "right" answer that children are afraid they will get wrong. For example: Why do you think John went to bed wearing his stockings and one shoe? What do you think John might have been doing that made him very tired? What do you wear on your feet when you go to bed?

- If you have a small enough group and adequate time, act out "Diddle Diddle Dumpling" with creative dramatics. Have several children at a time be "my son John" or "my girl Jane" while the other children chant the rhyme. Make sure that each child gets to play the role of John/Jane.

Letter Knowledge—Letter D *(Learn to recognize and identify letters, knowing that they have different names and sounds and that the same letter can look different.)*

- Show a large-size cutout or magnet-backed foam letter "D" and "d" (see Resources). Point to the capital "D" letters that begin the words "Diddle, Diddle" and "Dumpling" in the title of your poster. Say: "Here is the letter D—a big uppercase, or capital D." Draw the capital letter "D" in the air as a group. Point to a small letter "d" on the poster within the rhyme's text. Say: "Here is also the letter d—a small, lowercase d." Draw a lowercase "d" in the air as a group. Make the /D/ sound and say: "D is for Diddle Diddle; D is for Dumpling; D is for Dinosaur; D is for Duck; D is for Doughnut; D is for Dog; D is for Dance; D is for Doll; D is for Door; D is for Daddy." Encourage the audience to repeat each phrase after you. Include three or four examples.

- Demonstrate making the shapes of "D" and "d" using string or pipe cleaners.

Parent/Caregiver Connection

- Reinforce the parent/caregiver's key role in their child's early literacy development through comfortable, relaxed times together with songs, rhymes, and books. Emphasize fun and enjoyment as the goals.

- Encourage caregivers to participate during storytime and to incorporate "Diddle Diddle Dumpling" at home during play and reading times. Select one of the "Diddle Diddle Dumpling" early literacy activities that you share together during storytime, and briefly explain how the activity supports children's early literacy development. Suggest repeating the activity at home. Try different activities to highlight different skills during each storytime.

- Share information about Dialogic, or "Hear and Say" Reading (see Resources). Encourage parents and caregivers to individually discuss the day's rhyme, its characters, and events in an open-ended way with their children, following the child's interest while affirming and expanding upon their answers. For example, point to John in "Diddle Diddle Dumpling" and ask, "Who is this?" Child: "A boy." Follow up with positive affirmation, and enlarge: "Yes, it's a boy named John. What is he doing?" Child: "Sleeping." Expand: "Yes, the boy is sleeping in his bed." Help the child repeat longer phrases. Ask open-ended questions such as: "What do you see in this picture?" Build on the things that catch the child's interest. This type of positive, interactive discussion around familiar rhymes and books helps improve early language development, communication, and parent/child relationships.

Take-home "Diddle Diddle Dumpling"

Copy the "Diddle Diddle Dumpling" illustration from page 19 onto card stock and distribute. Color and cut out the piece at the end of storytime, or encourage the families to do so at home. Make a sample of the take-home version, and demonstrate singing or saying the rhyme using the small piece. (Families may affix sticky-back magnet material to pieces for playtime use on a magnetic surface such as a cookie sheet or the refrigerator if desired. Be aware of choking hazard considerations for younger children.)

Additional Extension Ideas

Note: For all craft activities, provide materials for adult attendees as well as children. Encourage children and adults to talk together about what they are making, and to use the completed crafts to retell or act out the rhyme.

- Show the pictures from several different nursery rhyme books that illustrate "Diddle Diddle Dumpling," and repeat the rhyme together with each new illustration. Talk about the differences between the various illustrations.

- Trace the children's feet on paper and cut out the outlines. Have the children use their foot outlines as shoe templates to decorate for John or for themselves. Ask the children: "What kind of shoes might John have especially liked?"

- Serve a bedtime "dumpling" snack for John. Since real dumplings are served hot, use plain doughnut holes for a substitute. Put the "dumplings" on a tray and carry it, calling "Diddle, diddle, diddle Dumpling!" like the dumpling sellers. Make some play dumplings from giant pom-poms and allow the children to take turns being the dumpling seller.

- Talk about what a "pair" means. Read *A Pair of Socks* by Stuart Murphy (HarperCollins, 1996), in which a sock searches the house for its lost mate. Play a sock-matching game, deciding as a group whether or not two particular socks make a pair. Manipulate the mateless sock as a puppet, singing the "Sock Song" to the tune of "Do You Know the Muffin Man?"

"Can you find my matching sock,
My matching sock, my matching sock?
Can you find my matching sock,
So I will be a pair?"

"Yes, we found your matching sock,
Your matching sock, your matching sock.

Yes, we found your matching sock,
So you will be a pair."

(Suggest that families and caregivers play matching games with their children using socks from the clean laundry, matching cards, or other items that are in pairs. Developing children's abilities to notice what is alike and different is one of the beginning steps toward letter knowledge.)

- Make a Sock Puppet craft. Glue felt, yarn, foamies, and wiggle eyes to brightly colored socks to create sock puppets (use "tacky" craft glue). Interview the puppets about their lives as socks before they became puppets. (For example, did they go to the park a lot? Did they get sandy? Did they get holes from playing outside? What were their favorite games? How did it feel to go in the washing machine? How about the dryer? And so forth.)

- Play a shoe-matching or shoe-memory game with real shoes or with paper shoe cutouts.

- Make the shapes of "D" and "d" using string, pipe cleaners, or clay.

Diddle Diddle Dumpling

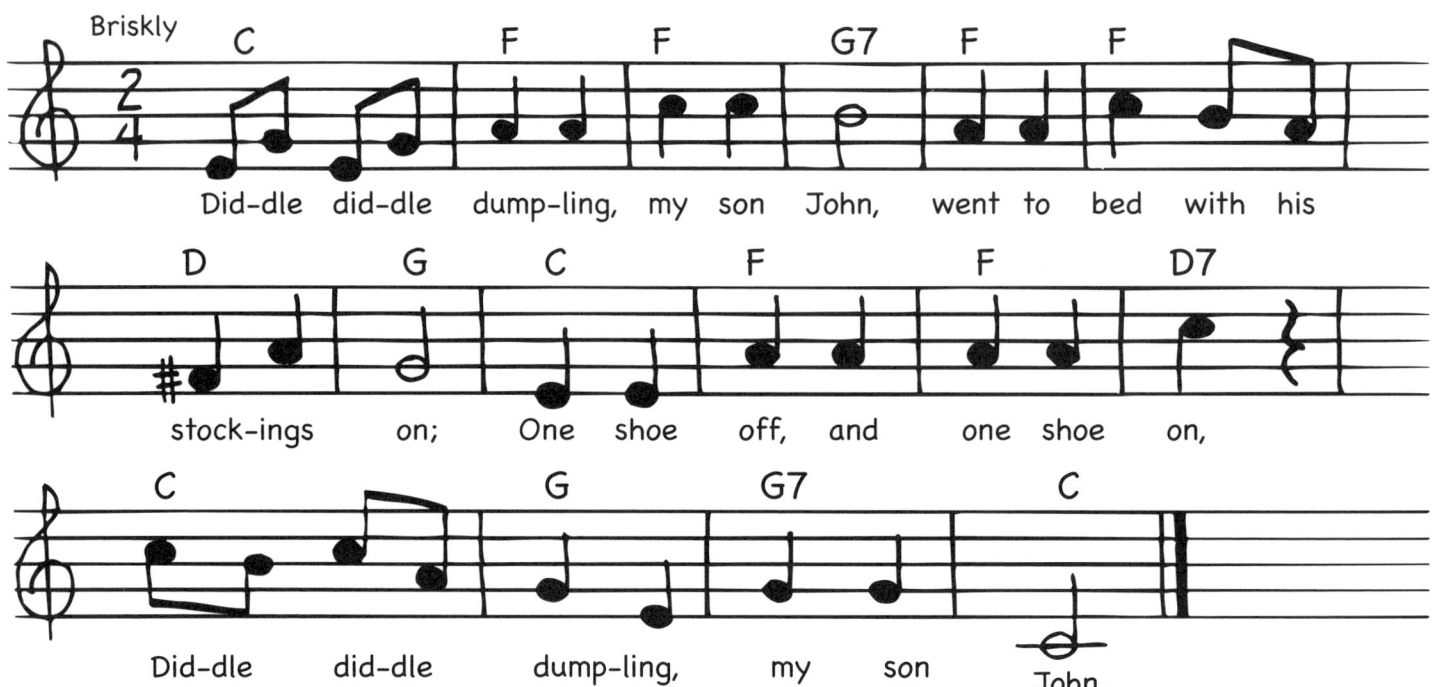

Take-home Diddle Diddle Dumpling

Diddle diddle dumpling, my son John,
Went to bed with his stockings on;
One shoe off, and one shoe on,
Diddle diddle dumpling, my son John.

Hey Diddle Diddle

> Hey diddle diddle,
>
> The cat and the fiddle,
>
> The cow jumped over the moon.
>
> The little dog laughed
>
> To see such fun,
>
> And the dish ran away with the spoon.

Variants

Alternate versions of this rhyme replace the word "fun" with "sport" or "a sight." The earliest printed version used "High diddle, diddle" and "To see such Craft."

History

Believed by many scholars to be the most well-known nonsense verse in the English language, "Hey Diddle Diddle's" origins have been the subject of much debate.

Some think that the cat refers to England's Queen Elizabeth I (1533–1603). The queen loved fiddle music, and her habit of toying with the court politicians earned her the nickname "the Cat." The little dog could be Robert Dudley, Earl of Leicester, whom Elizabeth referred to as her "little lapdog" and considered marrying. The dish and the spoon can be matched to an Elizabethan court couple, as well. A nobleman who carried the queen's golden dishes into the royal dining room was called "the dish," and a young woman who served as the royal food taster was called "the spoon." One such "dish," the Earl of Hertford, eloped with "spoon" Lady Katherine Grey during Elizabeth's reign.

Other scholars, including the Opies, discount this theory. The rhyme was definitely included in *Mother Goose's Melody* (c. 1765), however, and in 1882 Randolph Caldecott illustrated *Hey Diddle Diddle* as a popular picture book that was sold for one shilling.

Musical Notation

See musical notation on page 27.

Preparing and Using the Mother Goose Rhyme Time Pieces

"Hey Diddle Diddle" pieces:

- Cat with fiddle
- Jumping cow
- Laughing little dog
- Running dish and spoon
- Large moon with face (this moon will also be used for "The Man in the Moon" and "There Was an Old Woman Tossed Up in a Basket")
- "Hey Diddle Diddle" poster

Organize the "Hey Diddle Diddle" rhyme pieces ahead of time in the order in which they appear in the rhyme: the dish and spoon on the bottom of the stack, the little dog on top of them, the moon and cow on top of the little dog, and the cat and fiddle on the very top. Hide the stack out of sight.

Before sharing the rhyme, place the poster on an easel so the audience can see it clearly. Hold each rhyme piece up one at a time as you sing or say the rhyme. Don't forget to make the cow jump over the moon! Set each piece back down again, or affix the pieces successively to a large Velcro or magnet board. If you wish to incorporate motions or use a musical instrument for accompaniment, point to each piece on the board in turn as you lead the group in the actions or play and sing the song.

Utilize the sections of Mother Goose Rhyme Time that work best for you and your storytime group or classroom. Experiment with new ideas and techniques. Practice ahead of time so you feel comfortable with the material and can focus on the audience rather than on trying to remember how you intended to share the rhyme.

Storytime

Share "Hey Diddle Diddle" as a song or as a chant; rocking back and forth, bouncing, patting your lap, or clapping to keep a rhythm. Sing or say the rhyme quickly and slowly, loudly and quietly. Incorporate movements and animal noises as desired. Encourage the children's caregivers to adapt motions or make up new ones as appropriate for their child; many different actions are possible. Here are a few options:

Babies *(Sitting on caregivers' laps)*

> Hey diddle diddle, *(Gently bounce baby.)*
> The cat and the fiddle, *("Meow.")*
> The cow jumped OVER the moooooon.
> *(Lift baby UP in the air.)*
> The little dog laughed *(Laugh barkingly.)*
> To see such fun, *(Gently bounce baby.)*
> And the dish ran away with the spoon.
> *(Run fingers up baby's arm or leg and gently tickle baby.)*

Older Children *(Standing or sitting)*

> Hey diddle diddle,
> *(Clap hands rhythmically.)*
> The cat and the fiddle,
> *("Meow," then pretend to fiddle.)*
> The cow jumped OVER the mooooon.
> *(Jump up high while "mooing.")*
> The little dog laughed *(Laugh barkingly.)*
> To see such fun, *(Clap hands rhythmically.)*
> And the dish ran away with the spoon.
> *(Run in place or pat lap for running sound.)*

Early Literacy Activities

Consider integrating one or several of the activities or techniques suggested below as you share the nursery rhyme. All activities should be approached in a fun and playful manner, encouraging curiosity and allowing for children's individual differences. **Note:** Be aware of children's developmental stages and focus on the activities that are appropriate for the ages and stages of your group. The suggestions provided are intended to give you a variety of ideas to work with over time. You will not incorporate all of the techniques at once. Share one rhyme several times during a single storytime, and repeat the same rhyme over several storytimes. Try different activities to highlight a different skill during each storytime.

Print Motivation *(Encourage interest in and excitement about reading and books.)*

- Say the words rhythmically and with enthusiasm, conveying your enjoyment of the rhyme.

- Repeat the rhyme several times together with the children, encouraging their own enjoyment and internalization of its lively rhythms.

Language and Vocabulary *(Introduce and explain new words or new meanings to familiar words.)*

- Use the rhyme pieces to illustrate and help explain language and vocabulary. Pause momentarily as you point to familiar objects for the children to supply the name or word if they know it. Say: "The cat *(point to the cat)* is making music by playing a fiddle *(point*

to the fiddle), which is like a violin. The cow *(point to the cow)* jumped over the moon *(move the cow as if it is jumping over the moon)*. The little dog *(point to the dog)* laughed to see such fun, and the dish *(point to the dish)* ran away with the spoon *(point to the spoon).*"

- Talk or sing about the illustrations: "I see a cat." "I see a dog." Pause for the children to name the object to which you are pointing. "I see a _____." Expand on descriptive features of the illustrations to build vocabulary and encourage the children's awareness of and attention to details: "I see a dog. A dog that is laughing and wearing a collar."

Phonological Awareness *(Play with rhymes, practice breaking words apart and putting them back together, and listen for beginning sounds and alliteration.)*

- Play with the words, sounds, animals, and objects in the rhyme and change them. Use puppets or props to dramatize. For example:

  Hey doodle doodle,
  The cat ate a noodle,
  The horse jumped over a star.
  The little pig laughed to see such fun,
  And the forks drove away in a car.

- Explain that rhyming words sound the same at the end. "Diddle" and "fiddle"; "doodle" and "noodle"; "moon" and "spoon"; and "star" and "car" are all rhyming word pairs. Try pausing just before the end of a rhyming pair and encourage the children to supply the rhyming word (such as "noodle" and "car" above) with the support of visual clues or context, or simply through the sounds suggested by the rhyme.

- Blend word parts in a variety of ways.

  Syllables: o ... ver. What's the word? *(Over.)*

  Onset sound: /d/ ... og. What's the word? *(Dog.)* What other words start with /d/?

  Phoneme by phoneme (for older children, in primary grades): /m/-/oo/-/n/. What's the word? *(Moon.)*

- Practice segmenting or "stretching" the nursery rhyme words (for older children, in primary grades). Show the children a rubber band and stretch it out and in. As you stretch the rubber band out longer, you can see all of its parts more clearly. Explain that you can also stretch words, so that you can hear each individual sound (phoneme) in the word. Stretch the word "cat": /c/-/a/-/t/. Sometimes one phoneme is represented by more than one letter, such as in the word "moon": /m/-/oo/-/n/. "Moon" contains three phonemes. Stretch other nursery rhyme words.

- Clap words: Clap once for each word in the rhyme, following the poster. Introduce variety by stomping feet or jumping once for each word.

- Clap syllables: Older children can learn to clap once for each syllable in the rhyme. Practice with one word at a time as the children begin to understand the concept. For example: Hey (1 clap); did-dle (2 claps); did-dle (2 claps); the (1 clap); cat (1 clap); and (1 clap); the (1 clap); fid-dle (2 claps). Introduce variety by stomping feet or jumping to the syllables.

Print Awareness *(Notice print and know how to handle books and follow the written word on a page.)*

- Point to the "Hey Diddle Diddle" poster. Say: "Our nursery rhyme is written right up here. I'll read it aloud, and then we'll say it again together." Follow the text of the rhyme with your finger as you read the poster, from left to right.

- Occasionally turn the poster upside down or sideways and see if the children detect the problem.

Narrative Skills *(Practice retelling stories or events, sequencing the order in which events happened, and adding descriptions.)*

- Talk and ask two or three open-ended questions about the rhyme and the objects and characters in it, and allow the children to ask questions. Avoid asking yes/no questions unless there is a specific purpose in doing so. Qualify questions by including the phrase "do you think," as in "Why do you think ...?" or "What do you think ...?" This type of question does not have a "right" answer that children are afraid they will get wrong.

- Discuss the order in which things happen in the rhyme, and why they might have happened that way. Use the rhyme pieces as visual prompts if necessary. For example: Which animal do we hear about first in "Hey Diddle Diddle"? What is the cat doing? Why do you think the cat is doing that? Have you ever seen a cat play a fiddle in real life? Who do you think taught the cat to play the fiddle? Which animal comes along next? What does it look like the cow is doing? Do you think that could really happen? Why do you think the cow wants to jump over the moon? Do you think she is just going to jump over the moon, or is she going to stay on the moon for awhile? What do you think the cow would do on the moon? Which animal do we hear about next? What is the little dog doing? Why do you think the little dog is laughing? Would you laugh if you saw a cat playing a fiddle and a cow jumping over the moon? What happens next in the rhyme? Why do you think the dish and spoon are running away? Where might they be going? Where are the rest of the dishes and silverware? Do the dish and spoon belong to somebody in particular? **Note:** These are too many questions for one program; pick and choose the questions you plan to ask.

- If you have a small enough group and adequate time, act out "Hey Diddle Diddle" with creative dramatics. Have several children at a time be cats, cows, little dogs, and dishes with spoons. Make sure that each child gets to play all of the various roles if possible, and to choose who or what they want to be.

Letter Knowledge—Letter H *(Learn to recognize and identify letters, knowing that they have different names and sounds and knowing that the same letter can look different.)*

- Show a large-size cutout or magnet-backed foam letter "H" and "h" (see Resources). Point to the capital "H" letter that begins the word "Hey" in the title of your poster. Say: "Here is the letter H—a big uppercase, or capital H." Draw the capital letter "H" in the air as a group. Point to a small letter "h" on the poster within the rhyme's text. Say: "Here is also the letter h—a small, lowercase h." Draw a lowercase "h" in the air as a group. Make the breathy /H/ sound and say: "H is for Hey; H is for Hi; H is for House; H is for Head; H is for Hat; H is for Horse; H is for Hand; H is for Hop; H is for Hiccup; H is for Help; H is for Happy." Encourage the audience to repeat each phrase after you. Include three or four examples.

- Demonstrate making the shapes of "H" and "h" using string or pipe cleaners.

Parent/Caregiver Connection

- Reinforce the parent/caregiver's key role in their child's early literacy development through comfortable, relaxed times together with songs, rhymes, and books. Emphasize fun and enjoyment as the goals.

- Encourage caregivers to participate during storytime and to incorporate "Hey Diddle Diddle" at home during play and reading times. Select one of the "Hey Diddle Diddle" early literacy activities that you share together during storytime, and briefly explain how the activity supports children's early literacy development. Suggest repeating the activity at home. Try different activities to highlight different skills during each storytime.

- Share information about Dialogic, or "Hear and Say" Reading (see Resources). Encourage parents and caregivers to individually discuss the day's rhyme, its characters, and events in an open-ended way with their children, following the child's interest while affirming and expanding upon their answers. For example, point to the cow in "Hey Diddle Diddle" and ask, "What is this?" Child: "A cow." Follow up with positive affirmation, and enlarge: "Yes, it's a brown cow with brown spots. What is she doing?" Child: "Jumping." Expand: "Yes, she is jumping up

high, over the moon!" Help the child repeat longer phrases. Ask open-ended questions such as: "What do you see in this picture?" Build on the things that catch the child's interest. This type of positive, interactive discussion around familiar rhymes and books helps improve early language development, communication, and parent/child relationships.

Take-home "Hey Diddle Diddle"

Copy the "Hey Diddle Diddle" illustrations from pages 28–29 onto card stock and distribute. Color and cut out the pieces at the end of storytime, or encourage the families to do so at home. Glue or tape the moon securely onto a wide craft stick if desired. Make a sample of the take-home version, and demonstrate singing or saying the rhyme using the small pieces. (Families may affix sticky-back magnet material to pieces for playtime use on a magnetic surface such as a cookie sheet or the refrigerator if desired. Be aware of choking hazard considerations for younger children.)

Additional Extension Ideas

Note: For all craft activities, provide materials for adult attendees as well as children. Encourage children and adults to talk together about what they are making, and to use the completed crafts to retell or act out the rhyme.

- Show the pictures from several different nursery rhyme books that illustrate "Hey Diddle Diddle," and repeat the rhyme together with each new illustration. Talk about the differences between the various illustrations.

- Make a Runaway Dish-and-Spoon craft with paper or plastic picnic ware. Use a paper punch to make holes in the dish, and join it to the plastic spoon with pipe cleaners. Decorate the dish and spoon with faces, yarn hair, hands, and feet as desired.

- Make a Cow Jumping Over the Moon craft. Draw a jumping cow on the top edge of a piece of card stock, and outline a long, wide tab of blank paper below it that is slightly longer than the radius of a white paper plate. If you hold the cow so it shows above the edge of the paper plate, the tab should reach slightly past the plate's center. Cut out the cow with the long tab. Punch a small hole in the middle of the paper plate and near the bottom of the tab. Insert a metal brad through the plate and tab, so the cow can circle the paper plate moon.

- Make musical "fiddles" by stretching rubber bands around Styrofoam trays or shoebox bottoms. Add a ruler or craft stick neck and decorate as desired.

- Talk about: The different phases of the moon. Sometimes we can see the full moon whole and round, sometimes a gibbous moon not quite round, sometimes just half, or a sliver of the crescent moon. Flatten large white basket coffee filters and mottle them with watercolor paints. Allow the filters to dry completely, then cut them into various phases of the moon.

- Make a giant paper crescent moon and lay it on the floor. Line up and jump over it while saying the "Hey Diddle Diddle" rhyme.

- Allow each child to decide upon their favorite "Hey Diddle Diddle" character, then make paper plate animal or moon masks or stick puppets. Instructions for stick puppets are included in *A Pocketful of Puppets: Mother Goose* by Tamara Hunt and Nancy Renfro (Nancy Renfro Studios, 1998), or design your own.

- Make a Runaway Dish and Spoon Puppet. Complete instructions are included in *Crafts From Your Favorite Nursery Rhymes* by Kathy Ross (Millbrook Press, 2002).

- Read *And the Dish Ran Away With the Spoon* by Janet Stevens and Susan Stevens Crummel (Harcourt, 2001). Each night when the "Hey Diddle Diddle" rhyme is read, Dish and Spoon run away as directed, then return to run away again the following evening. When Dish and Spoon fail to return one fateful night, however, the rhyme's cat, cow, and dog set out to find them.

- Read *Mrs. Mooley* by Jack Kent (Golden Books Publishing Company, Inc., 2002, 1973). Mrs. Mooley the cow sees a picture of

a cow jumping over the moon in a nursery rhyme book, and determines to embark on such an adventure herself despite her disbelieving barnyard companions.

- Read *Two Cool Cows* by Toby Speed (Putnam, 1995). Millie and Maude are two cool cows who fly to the moon and back in a night wearing the Huckabuck children's new black boots.

- Read the Big Book edition (see Resources) of *Goodnight Moon* by Margaret Wise Brown; pictures by Clement Hurd (Scholastic, 1975). A little bunny says goodnight to each of the objects in the great green room, including a picture of a cow jumping over the moon as well as kittens, mittens, clocks, socks, and more. Encourage the children to find the picture of the cow jumping over the moon throughout the story.

- Share "Old King Cole and the Cat and the Fiddle" "in two voices" from *You Read to Me, I'll Read to You: Very Short Mother Goose Tales to Read Together* by Mary Ann Hoberman and illustrated by Michael Emberley (Little, Brown and Company, 2005). Before you begin, familiarize the children with the standard version of "Old King Cole" from a classic Mother Goose rhyme book.

- Make the shapes of "H" and "h" using string, pipe cleaners, or clay.

Hey Diddle Diddle

Take-home Hey Diddle Diddle

Hey diddle diddle,

The cat and the fiddle,

The cow jumped over the moon.

The little dog laughed

To see such fun,

And the dish ran away with the spoon.

Hey Diddle Diddle Mother Goose Rhyme Time: Night 29

Jack Be Nimble

> Jack be nimble,
> Jack be quick,
> Jack jump over
> The candlestick.

Variants

Some versions of this rhyme append the following:

> Jack jumped up high,
> Jack jumped down low.
> Jack jumped over
> And burned his toe.

On Bob McGrath's *Songs & Games for Toddlers* (Bob's Kids Music, 2000) and *The Baby Record* (Bob's Kids Music, 2000).

Also see Bruce Lansky's clever twist on the rhyme in *Mary Had a Little Jam and Other Silly Rhymes,* where Jack keeps jumping much too close and ends up with his pants smelling like burnt toast!

Lansky, Bruce. *Mary Had a Little Jam and Other Silly Rhymes.* Meadowbrook Press, 2004. Formerly titled: *The New Adventures of Mother Goose: Gentle Rhymes for Happy Times* (Meadowbrook Press, 1993).

The occasional name substitution occurs historically, such as the replacement of "Jack" with "Kit" in a mid-twentieth-century publication.

History

"Jack Be Nimble" was likely inspired by the historical English game of "candle-leaping," practiced as early as the 1600s. The game, which involved a candlestick with a lighted candle being placed on the floor of a room, was a combination of sport and superstitious fortune telling. A person who could jump over the candle without extinguishing the flame would supposedly be rewarded with an entire year of good luck. Candlestick jumping was a particular highlight of some villages' St. Catherine's Day (November 25) celebrations.

Musical Notation

See musical notation on page 36.

Preparing and Using the Mother Goose Rhyme Time Pieces

"Jack Be Nimble" pieces:

- Jumping boy
- Candlestick with candle
- "Jack Be Nimble" poster

Before sharing the rhyme, place the poster on an easel so the audience can see it clearly. Hold Jack in one hand and the candlestick in the other, or affix the candlestick to a Velcro or magnet board. Actions for the rhyme are very simple, so you should be able to hold Jack throughout the rhyme and jump with him or bounce him on your lap. If you wish to use a musical instrument for accompaniment, place Jack on the board along with the candlestick, and point to him as you play and sing the song.

Utilize the sections of Mother Goose Rhyme Time that work best for you and your storytime group or classroom. Experiment with new ideas and techniques. Practice ahead of time so you feel comfortable with the material and can focus on the audience rather than on trying to remember how you intended to share the rhyme.

Storytime

Share "Jack Be Nimble" as a song or as a chant; bouncing, patting your lap, or clapping to keep a rhythm. Sing or say the rhyme quickly and slowly, loudly and quietly. Incorporate movements as desired, particularly jumping! Children who are unable to jump may optionally fling their arms in the air on the word "over."

Babies *(Sitting on caregivers' laps)*

> Jack be nimble,
> *(Bounce baby on knees or clap for rhythm.)*
> Jack be quick,
> Jack jump over
> *(Lift baby up in the air or over to other knee.)*
> The candlestick.
> *(Bounce baby on knees or clap for rhythm.)*

Older Children *(Standing)*

> Jack be nimble,
> *(Clap or pat lap rhythmically.)*
> Jack be quick,
> Jack jump over
> *(Jump up high on "OVER.")*
> The candlestick.
> *(Clap or pat lap rhythmically.)*
>
> (**Note:** *Parents can make a fist with their thumb up for the "candle" while the child jumps over it.)*

Early Literacy Activities

Consider integrating several of the activities or techniques suggested below as you share the nursery rhyme. All activities should be approached in a fun and playful manner, encouraging curiosity and allowing for children's individual differences. **Note:** Be aware of children's developmental stages and focus on the activities that are appropriate for the ages and stages of your group. The suggestions provided are intended to give you a variety of ideas to work with over time. You will not incorporate all of the techniques at once. Share one rhyme several times during a single storytime, and repeat the same rhyme over several storytimes. Try different activities to highlight a different skill during each storytime.

Print Motivation *(Encourage interest in and excitement about reading and books.)*

- Say the words rhythmically and with enthusiasm, conveying your enjoyment of the rhyme.

- Repeat the rhyme several times together with the children, encouraging their own enjoyment and internalization of its lively rhythms.

Language and Vocabulary *(Introduce and explain new words or new meanings to familiar words.)*

- Use the rhyme pieces to illustrate and help explain language and vocabulary. Pause momentarily as you point to each object for the children to supply the name or word if they know it. Say: "This boy's name is Jack *(point to Jack)*. We are telling him to be nimble, which means to keep his body all coordinated together so he can do the job quickly and well. We also are telling him to be quick—he needs to jump fast! Jack is jumping over a candlestick *(point to the rhyme piece candlestick)*, which holds a candle *(point to the candle)* so the candle will stand up straight and not fall over."

- Talk or sing about the illustrations: "I see a candle." "I see a candlestick." Pause for the children to name the object to which you are pointing: "I see a _____." Expand on descriptive features of the illustrations to build vocabulary and encourage the children's awareness of and attention to details: "I see a boy. A boy who is jumping with his arms in the air."

Phonological Awareness (*Play with rhymes, practice breaking words apart and putting them back together, and listen for beginning sounds and alliteration.*)

- Play with the words, names, and objects in the rhyme and change them. Use puppets or props to dramatize. For example, change the object that Jack jumps over: The big red brick, the long blue stick, and so forth. Change Jack's demeanor, such as "Jack be sleepy / Jack be slow / Jack jump over / The big red bow."

- Explain that rhyming words sound the same at the end, giving examples. Try pausing just before the end of a rhyming pair and encourage the children to supply the rhyming word (such as "bow" above) with the support of visual clues or context, or simply through the sounds suggested by the rhyme.

- Play an "oddity task" game. For example, which word does not rhyme? Quick, stick, nimble. (*Answer: nimble.*) Which word sounds different at the beginning? Jack, over, jump. (*Answer: over.*)

- Blend word parts in a variety of ways.

  Syllables: nim ... ble. What's the word? (*Nimble.*)

  Onset sound: /j/ ... ump. What's the word? (*Jump.*) What other words start with /j/?

- Phoneme by phoneme (for older children, in primary grades): /J/-/a/-/ck/. What's the word? (*Jack.*)

- Practice segmenting or "stretching" the nursery rhyme words (for older children, in primary grades). Show the children a rubber band and stretch it out and in. As you stretch the rubber band out longer, you can see all of its parts more clearly. Explain that you can also stretch words, so that you can hear each individual sound (phoneme) in the word. Stretch the word "jump": /j/-/u/-/m/-/p/. Sometimes one phoneme is represented by more than one letter, such as in the name "Jack": /J/-/a/-/ck/. "Jack" contains three phonemes. Stretch other nursery rhyme words.

- Clap words: Clap once for each word in the rhyme, following the poster. Introduce variety by stomping feet or jumping once for each word.

- Clap syllables: Older children can learn to clap once for each syllable in the rhyme. Practice with one word at a time as the children begin to understand the concept. For example: Jack (1 clap); be (1 clap); nim-ble (2 claps); Jack (1 clap); be (1 clap); quick (1 clap). Introduce variety by stomping feet or jumping to the syllables.

Print Awareness (*Notice print and know how to handle books and follow the written word on a page.*)

- Point to the "Jack Be Nimble" poster. Say: "Our nursery rhyme is written right up here. I'll read it aloud, and then we'll say it again together." Follow the text of the rhyme with your finger as you read the poster, from left to right.

- Occasionally turn the poster upside down or sideways and see if the children detect the problem.

Narrative Skills (*Practice retelling stories or events, sequencing the order in which events happened, and adding descriptions.*)

- Talk and ask questions about the rhyme, and allow the children to ask questions. For example: What is happening in the rhyme? To whom are we saying the rhyme? What are we telling Jack to do? Why does Jack need to be nimble and quick? How is he jumping? Around? Under? Over? What is he jumping over? Use the rhyme pieces as visual prompts if necessary. What was the biggest thing you have ever jumped over?

- If you have a small enough group and adequate time, act out "Jack Be Nimble" with creative dramatics. Change the name "Jack" to each of the children's names in turn as they jump over a pretend candlestick.

Letter Knowledge—Letter N (*Learn to recognize and identify letters, knowing that they have different names and sounds and that the same letter can look different.*)

- Show a large-size cutout or magnet-backed foam letter "N" and "n" (see Resources). Point to the capital "N" letter that begins the word "Nimble" in the title of your poster. Say: "Here is the letter N—a big uppercase, or capital N." Draw the capital letter "N" in the air as a group. Point to the small letter "n" on the poster within the rhyme's text. Say: "Here is also the letter n—a small, lowercase n." Draw a lowercase "n" in the air as a group. Make the /N/ sound and say: "N is for Nimble; N is for Nice; N is for Neck; N is for Nose; N is for Nap; N is for No; and N is for Neighbor." Encourage the audience to repeat each phrase after you. Include three or four examples.

- Demonstrate making the shapes of "N" and "n" using string or pipe cleaners.

Parent/Caregiver Connection

- Reinforce the parent/caregiver's key role in their child's early literacy development through comfortable, relaxed times together with songs, rhymes, and books. Emphasize fun and enjoyment as the goals.

- Encourage caregivers to participate during storytime and to incorporate "Jack Be Nimble" at home during play and reading times. Select one of the "Jack Be Nimble" early literacy activities that you share together during storytime, and briefly explain how the activity supports children's early literacy development. Suggest repeating the activity at home. Try different activities to highlight different skills during each storytime.

- Share information about Dialogic, or "Hear and Say" Reading (see Resources). Encourage parents and caregivers to individually discuss the day's rhyme, its characters, and events in an open-ended way with their children, following the child's interest while affirming and expanding upon their answers. For example, point to Jack in "Jack Be Nimble" and ask, "Who is this?" Child: "A boy." Follow up with positive affirmation, and enlarge: "Yes, it's a boy named Jack. What is he doing?" Child: "Jumping." Expand: "Yes, he is jumping over a candlestick." Help the child repeat longer phrases. Ask open-ended questions such as: "What do you see in this picture?" Build on the things that catch the child's interest. This type of positive, interactive discussion around familiar rhymes and books helps improve early language development, communication, and parent/child relationships.

Take-home "Jack Be Nimble"

Copy the "Jack Be Nimble" illustrations from page 37 onto card stock and distribute. Color and cut out the pieces at the end of storytime, or encourage the families to do so at home. Make a sample of the take-home version, and demonstrate singing or saying the rhyme using the small pieces. (Families may affix sticky-back magnet material to pieces for playtime use on a magnetic surface such as a cookie sheet or the refrigerator if desired. Be aware of choking hazard considerations for younger children.)

Additional Extension Ideas

Note: For all craft activities, provide materials for adult attendees as well as children. Encourage children and adults to talk together about what they are making, and to use the completed crafts to retell or act out the rhyme.

- Show the pictures from several different nursery rhyme books that illustrate "Jack Be Nimble," and repeat the rhyme together with each new illustration. Talk about the differences between the various illustrations.

- Talk about: The history of candle jumping (see page 31). The "Jack Be Nimble" rhyme is fun to pretend, but it would be dangerous and not a good idea in real life!

- Make a Jack's Candlestick craft. Have the children each decorate a paper towel or toilet paper tube "candle," and then twist red, yellow, and orange tissue paper so it comes out of the tube's top as the "flame." Glue or tape the "candles" to small-size paper plate "candleholders" for stability. Act out the rhyme.

- Make Jack Box Puppets. Complete instructions are included in *A Pocketful of Puppets: Mother Goose* by Tamara Hunt and Nancy Renfro (Nancy Renfro Studios, 1998), or design your own!

- Share "Jack, Be Nimble" "in two voices" from *You Read to Me, I'll Read to You: Very Short Mother Goose Tales to Read Together* by Mary Ann Hoberman (Little, Brown and Company, 2005).

- Make the shapes of "N" and "n" using string, pipe cleaners, or clay.

Jack Be Nimble

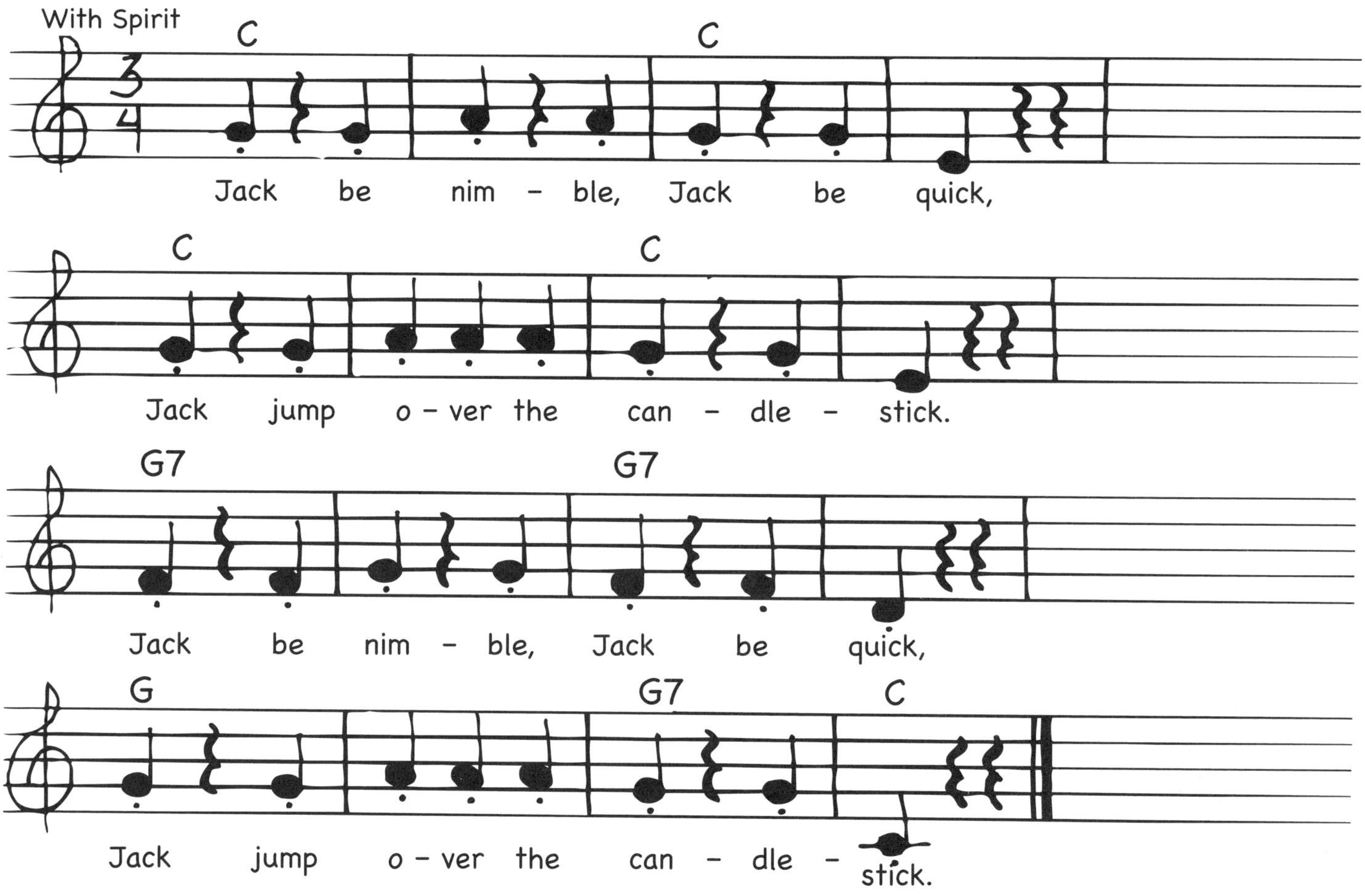
With Spirit
C C
Jack be nim - ble, Jack be quick,
C C
Jack jump o – ver the can - dle - stick.
G7 G7
Jack be nim - ble, Jack be quick,
G G7 C
Jack jump o – ver the can - dle - stick.

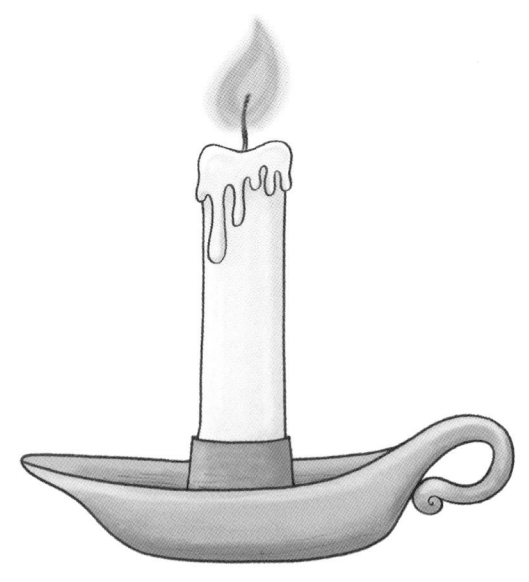

Take-home Jack Be Nimble

> Jack be nimble,
> Jack be quick,
> Jack jump over
> The candlestick.

Little Boy Blue

> Little Boy Blue,
>
> Come blow your horn.
>
> The sheep's in the meadow,
>
> The cow's in the corn.
>
> Where is the boy
>
> Who looks after the sheep?
>
> He's under a haystack,
>
> Fast asleep.

Variants

Some versions of this rhyme add the following:

"Will you wake him?"
"No, not I,
For if I do,
He's sure to cry."

The haystack is also variably referred to as a "haycock" or "hayrick."

History

"Little Boy Blue" may have represented Thomas, Cardinal Wolsey, chief minister for King Henry VIII. Wolsey was the son of a wealthy butcher, and probably looked after his father's livestock as a child. Wolsey acquired immense political power and wealth through his connection to the king, and is possibly being accused of "sleeping on the job," or paying more attention to social maneuvering than to his wandering religious subjects. The rhyme may also have either imitated or inspired a speech in Shakespeare's *King Lear* (Act III, Scene VI): "Sleepest or wakest thou, jolly shepherd? / Thy sheep be in the corn; / And for one blast of thy minikin mouth / Thy sheep shall take no harm."

Musical Notation

See musical notation on page 44.

Preparing and Using the Mother Goose Rhyme Time Pieces

"Little Boy Blue" pieces:

- Double-layered haystack with sleeping Little Boy Blue
- Sheep
- Cows
- "Little Boy Blue" poster

Organize the "Little Boy Blue" rhyme pieces ahead of time in the order in which they appear in the rhyme: the cow on the bottom of the stack, the sheep on top of the cow, and Little

Boy Blue's double-layered haystack on the very top. Hide the pieces out of sight.

Before sharing the rhyme, place the poster on an easel so the audience can see it clearly. Hold Little Boy Blue's haystack in one hand throughout the rhyme. With your other hand, hold up the sheep and then the cows. When you say "under," swivel the top plain haystack up and out to one side to reveal the slumbering Little Boy Blue. You may also affix the pieces successively to a large Velcro or magnet board. If you wish to incorporate motions or use a musical instrument for accompaniment, point to each piece on the board in turn as you lead the group in the actions or play and sing the song.

Utilize the sections of Mother Goose Rhyme Time that work best for you and your storytime group or classroom. Experiment with new ideas and techniques. Practice ahead of time so you feel comfortable with the material and can focus on the audience rather than on trying to remember how you intended to share the rhyme.

Storytime

Share "Little Boy Blue" as a song or as a chant; rocking back and forth, bouncing, patting your lap, or clapping to keep a rhythm. Sing or say the rhyme quickly and slowly, loudly and quietly. Incorporate movements, animal noises, shhh-hhing, and snoring as desired. Encourage the children's caregivers to adapt motions or make up new ones as appropriate for their child; many different actions are possible. Here are a few options:

Babies *(Sitting on caregivers' laps)*

> Little Boy Blue,
> *(Rock baby back and forth.)*
> Come blow your horn.
> The sheep's in the meadow,
> *(Tickle one of baby's palms and say "Baaa.")*
> The cow's in the corn.
> *(Tickle baby's other palm and say "Moo.")*
> Where is the boy
> *(Hands out, questioning.)*
> Who looks after the sheep?
> He's under a haystack,
> *(Tickle under baby's arm OR lift up baby's shirt and snuggle tummy.)*
> Fast asleep.

Older Children *(Standing or sitting)*

> Little Boy Blue,
> Come blow your horn.
> *(Pretend to toot horn, "Toot-a-loo!")*
> The sheep's in the meadow,
> *("Baaa.")*
> The cow's in the corn.
> *("Mooo.")*
> Where is the boy
> *(Hands out, questioning.)*
> Who looks after the sheep?
> He's under a haystack,
> *(Cover head with arms.)*
> Fast asleep.
> *(Head on hands, snore loudly.)*

Early Literacy Activities

Consider integrating several of the activities or techniques suggested below as you share the nursery rhyme. All activities should be approached in a fun and playful manner, encouraging curiosity and allowing for children's individual differences. **Note:** Be aware of children's developmental stages and focus on the activities that are appropriate for the ages and stages of your group. The suggestions provided are intended to give you a variety of ideas to work with over time. You will not incorporate all of the techniques at once. Share one rhyme several times during a single storytime, and repeat the same rhyme over several storytimes. Try different activities to highlight a different skill during each storytime.

Print Motivation *(Encourage interest in and excitement about reading and books.)*

- Say the words rhythmically and with enthusiasm, conveying your enjoyment of the rhyme.

- Repeat the rhyme several times together with the children, encouraging their own enjoyment and internalization of its lyrical rhythms.

Language and Vocabulary *(Introduce and explain new words or new meanings to familiar words.)*

- Use the rhyme pieces to illustrate and help explain language and vocabulary. Pause momentarily as you point to familiar objects for the children to supply the name or word if they know it. Say: "Little Boy Blue (*point to Little Boy Blue*) is sleeping under the haystack (*point to the haystack*). A haystack is a big stack or pile of hay. Farmers make hay by cutting and then drying out long grass or other plants like alfalfa or clover. The animals eat the dried hay during the winter, when there isn't fresh grass to eat. Little Boy Blue has a horn (*point to the horn*) to blow to call the sheep (*point to the sheep*) and the cows (*point to the cows*). The sheep and cows have wandered away from where they are supposed to be, and the cows are eating up the farmer's corn (*point to the corn*)! Little Boy Blue is 'fast asleep'—that means he is sound asleep. He's not just taking a tiny little nap, where he will wake up quickly if he hears the sheep or cows—he's sleeping like he would sleep when he goes to bed at night."

- Talk or sing about the illustrations: "I see a cow." "I see a sheep." Pause for the children to name the object to which you are pointing: "I see a _____." Expand on descriptive features of the illustrations to build vocabulary and encourage the children's awareness of and attention to details: "I see a boy. A boy wearing a blue hat and blue clothes."

Phonological Awareness (*Play with rhymes, practice breaking words apart and putting them back together, and listen for beginning sounds and alliteration.*)

- Play with the words, colors, animals, and objects in the rhyme and change them. Use puppets or props to dramatize. For example:

    Little Girl Pink,
    Come beat your drum.
    The sheep's making pancakes,
    The cow's chewing gum.
    Where is the girl
    Who looks after the sheep?
    She's under an apple tree,
    Fast asleep.

- Explain that rhyming words sound the same at the end. "Horn" and "corn" rhyme, as do "drum" and "gum," and "sheep" and "asleep." Try pausing just before the end of a rhyming pair and encourage the children to supply the rhyming word (such as "gum" and "asleep") with the support of visual clues or context, or simply through the sounds suggested by the rhyme.

- Blend word parts in a variety of ways.

    <u>Syllables</u>: hay ... stack. What's the word? (*Haystack.*)

    <u>Onset sound</u>: /b/ ... oy. What's the word? (*Boy.*) What other words start with /b/?

    <u>Phoneme by phoneme (for older children, in primary grades)</u>: /h/-/o/-/r/-/n/. What's the word? (*Horn.*)

- Practice segmenting or "stretching" the nursery rhyme words (for older children, in primary grades). Show the children a rubber band and stretch it out and in. As you stretch the rubber band out longer, you can see all of its parts more clearly. Explain that you can also stretch words, so that you can hear each individual sound (phoneme) in the word. Stretch the word "in": /i/-/n/. Sometimes one phoneme is represented by more than one letter, such as in the word "sheep": /sh/-/ee/-/p/. "Sheep" contains three phonemes. Stretch other nursery rhyme words.

- Clap words: Clap once for each word in the rhyme, following the poster. Introduce variety by stomping feet or jumping once for each word.

- Clap syllables: Older children can learn to clap once for each syllable in the rhyme. Practice with one word at a time as the children begin to understand the concept. For example: Lit-tle (2 claps); Boy (1 clap); Blue (1 clap); Come (1 clap); blow (1 clap); your (1 clap); horn (1 clap). Introduce variety by stomping feet or jumping to the syllables.

Print Awareness (*Notice print and know how to handle books and follow the written word on a page.*)

- Point to the "Little Boy Blue" poster. Say: "Our nursery rhyme is written right up here. I'll read it aloud, and then we'll say it again together." Follow the text of the rhyme with your finger as you read the poster, from left to right.

- Occasionally turn the poster upside down or sideways and see if the children detect the problem.

Narrative Skills *(Practice retelling stories or events, sequencing the order in which events happened, and adding descriptions.)*

- Talk and ask two or three open-ended questions about the rhyme and the objects and characters in it, and allow the children to ask questions. Avoid asking yes/no questions unless there is a specific purpose in doing so. Qualify questions by including the phrase "do you think," as in "Why do you think …?" or "What do you think …?" This type of question does not have a "right" answer that children are afraid they will get wrong. For example: Why do you think the boy was called "Little Boy Blue"? Why do you think Little Boy Blue would need to blow his horn? What do you think the sheep and the cows are doing out there in the meadow and in the corn? Why doesn't Little Boy Blue know what is happening? Why do you think he is sleeping under a haystack? What might he have been doing that made him feel so tired? When do you feel tired? **Note:** These are too many questions for one program; pick and choose the questions you plan to ask.

- If you have a small enough group and adequate time, act out "Little Boy Blue" with creative dramatics. Make a haystack by draping a blanket over a table. Have several children at a time hide under the table as the sleeping Little Boy/Girl Blue while the others take turns as sheep and cows. Make sure that each child gets to play all of the different roles if possible, and to choose who or what they want to be.

Letter Knowledge—Letter B *(Learn to recognize and identify letters, knowing that they have different names and sounds and that the same letter can look different.)*

- Show a large-size cutout or magnet-backed foam letter "B" and "b" (see Resources). Point to the capital "B" letters that begin the words "Boy" and "Blue" in the title of your poster. Say: "Here is the letter B—a big uppercase, or capital B." Draw the capital letter "B" in the air as a group. Point to a small letter "b" on the poster within the rhyme's text. Say "Here is also the letter b—a small, lowercase b." Draw a lowercase "b" in the air as a group. Make the /B/ sound and say: "B is for Boy; B is for Blue; B is for Bed; B is for Ball; B is for Bike; B is for Bear; B is for Balloon; B is for Baby; B is for Book." Encourage the audience to repeat each phrase after you. Include three or four examples.

- Demonstrate making the shapes of "B" and "b" using string or pipe cleaners.

Parent/Caregiver Connection

- Reinforce the parent/caregiver's key role in their child's early literacy development through comfortable, relaxed times together with songs, rhymes, and books. Emphasize fun and enjoyment as the goals.

- Encourage caregivers to participate during storytime and to incorporate "Little Boy Blue" at home during play and reading times. Select one of the "Little Boy Blue" early literacy activities that you share together during storytime, and briefly explain how the activity supports children's early literacy development. Suggest repeating the activity at home. Try different activities to highlight different skills during each storytime.

- Share information about Dialogic, or "Hear and Say" Reading (see Resources). Encourage parents and caregivers to individually discuss the day's rhyme, its characters, and events in an open-ended way with their children, following the child's interest while affirming and expanding upon their answers. For example, point to the boy in "Little Boy Blue" and ask, "Who is this?" Child: "A boy." Follow up with positive affirmation, and enlarge: "Yes, it's a boy wearing blue clothes, named Little Boy Blue. What

is he doing?" Child: "Sleeping." Expand: "Yes, he is sleeping under a haystack." Help the child repeat longer phrases. Ask open-ended questions such as: "What do you see in this picture?" Build on the things that catch the child's interest. This type of positive, interactive discussion around familiar rhymes and books helps improve early language development, communication, and parent/child relationships.

Take-home "Little Boy Blue"

Copy the "Little Boy Blue" illustrations from pages 45–47 onto card stock and distribute. Color, cut out, and assemble the pieces at the end of storytime, or encourage the families to do so at home. Fasten the plain front of the haystack to the back haystack piece at the dot. Use a metal brad fastener or knotted yarn so that the front can swivel out to the side. Make a sample of the take-home version, and demonstrate singing or saying the rhyme using the small pieces. (Families may affix sticky-back magnet material to pieces for playtime use on a magnetic surface such as a cookie sheet or the refrigerator if desired. Be aware of choking hazard considerations for younger children.)

Additional Extension Ideas

Note: For all craft activities, provide materials for adult attendees as well as children. Encourage children and adults to talk together about what they are making, and to use the completed crafts to retell or act out the rhyme.

- Show the pictures from several different nursery rhyme books that illustrate "Little Boy Blue," and repeat the rhyme together with each new illustration. Talk about the differences between the various illustrations.

- Make Little Boy Blue or Little Girl Blue hats from blue paper or blue plastic picnic bowls and decorate with blue crayons, blue star stickers, blue feathers, and so forth.

- Talk about: What if the boy was "Little Boy Green" or "Little Boy Purple"? Cut out variously colored clothes for Little Boy Blue. Make sure the rhyme figure is laminated so the clothes may be safely affixed to him with rolled-up masking or painter's tape. Say the rhyme with Little Boy Blue's new color each time.

- Make a Little Boy Blue's Horn craft with paper towel tubes. Cover the outside of the tubes with colored paper and decorate. Make pretend finger pads with round stickers. Play the horns by blowing into one end. Form a Little Boy/Girl Blue Marching Band wearing your blue paper hats and playing your horns.

- Make a Box Haystack and Little Boy Blue Paper Puppet to hide beneath it. Instructions are included in *A Pocketful of Puppets: Mother Goose* by Tamara Hunt and Nancy Renfro (Nancy Renfro Studios, 1998), or design your own.

- Make a Horn-Blowing Little Boy Blue. Complete instructions are included in *Crafts From Your Favorite Nursery Rhymes* by Kathy Ross (Millbrook Press, 2002).

- Share "Little Boy Blue and Little Bo-Peep" "in two voices" from *You Read to Me, I'll Read to You: Very Short Mother Goose Tales to Read Together* by Mary Ann Hoberman (Little, Brown and Company, 2005). Before you begin, familiarize the children with the standard version of "Little Bo-Peep" from a classic Mother Goose rhyme book or from *Mother Goose Rhyme Time: People*.

- Make the shapes of "B" and "b" using string, pipe cleaners, or clay.

Little Boy Blue

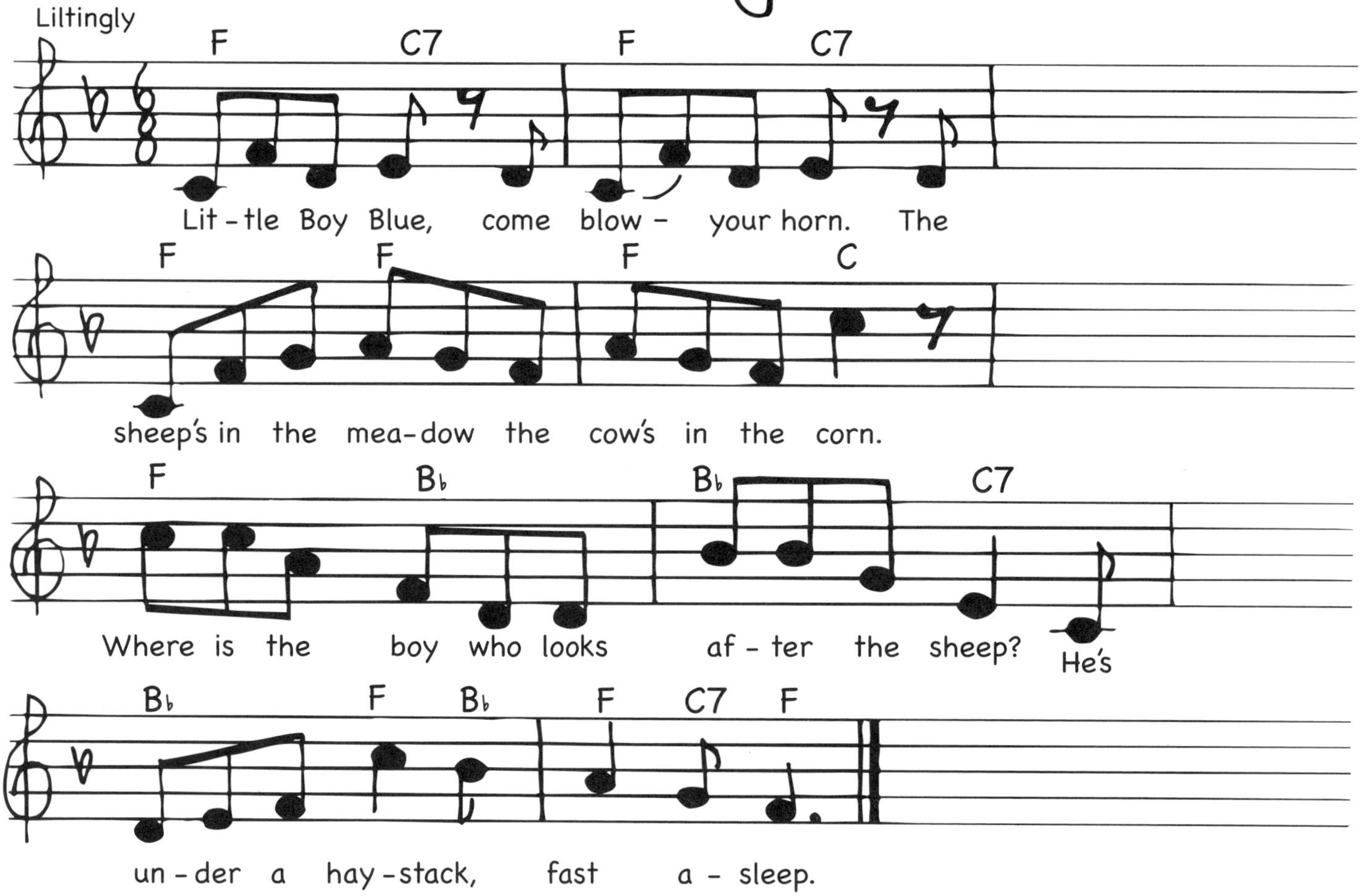
Liltingly
F C7 F C7
Lit-tle Boy Blue, come blow- your horn. The
F F F C
sheep's in the mea-dow the cow's in the corn.
F B♭ B♭ C7
Where is the boy who looks af-ter the sheep? He's
B♭ F B♭ F C7 F
un-der a hay-stack, fast a-sleep.

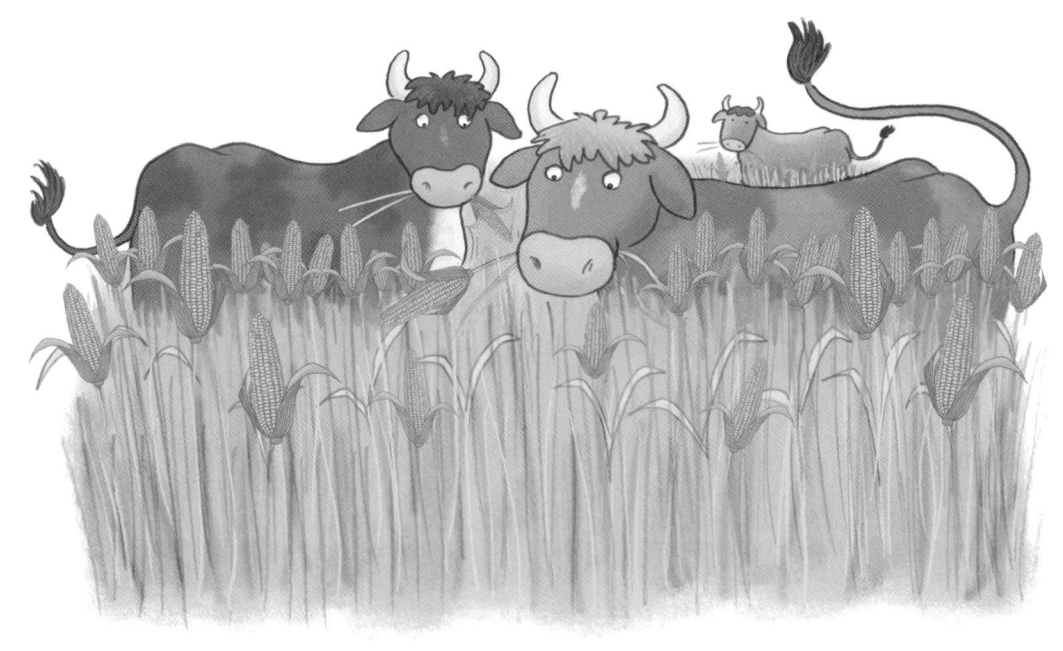

Take-home Little Boy Blue

Little Boy Blue,
Come blow your horn.
The sheep's in the meadow,
The cow's in the corn.
Where is the boy
Who looks after the sheep?
He's under a haystack,
Fast asleep.

Little Boy Blue Mother Goose Rhyme Time: Night 47

The Man in the Moon

> The Man in the Moon
> Looked out of the moon,
> Looked out of the moon and said:
> "It's time for all these children on the earth
> To think about going to bed!"

Variants

Several minor variations are:

"'Tis time for all children on the earth
To think about getting to bed!"

"'Tis time that, now I'm getting up,
All children/babies are in bed."

"It's time, I think, for all good children
To think about going to bed."

The Man in the Moon
Looked out of the moon,
And this is what he said,
"Now that I'm getting up, it's time
All children/babies went to bed."

History

The moon is an enduring presence in children's literature, and appears in countless nursery rhymes, stories, and childhood songs. The moon personified by the "Man in the Moon" appears frequently as well, in popular folk songs such as "Aikendrum" and in numerous other nursery rhymes such as the following:

The Man in the Moon
Came down too soon,
And asked his way to Norwich;
He went by the south,
And burnt his mouth
With supping cold plum porridge.

Although a historical identity for our bedtime rhyme's "Man in the Moon" has not been established, it seems clear that many moon-adoring young children might be willing to pay attention to his bedtime counsel.

Musical Notation

See musical notation on page 55.

Preparing and Using the Mother Goose Rhyme Time Pieces

"The Man in the Moon" pieces

- Large moon with face (this moon will also be used for "Hey Diddle Diddle" and "There Was an Old Woman Tossed Up in a Basket")

- "The Man in the Moon" poster

The moon may be used exactly as it is and held in your hands, or it may be glued or taped securely to a thick dowel rod or paint stirrer to create a giant moon stick puppet. If you choose

to leave the moon as it is, you may wish to display it high (but still within your reach) on a wall or hang it from the ceiling with a paper clip attached to fishing line.

Before sharing the rhyme, place the poster on an easel so the audience can see it clearly. Hold the moon up and make it bob about as if it was talking as you say or sing the rhyme. Sing or say the moon's lines in a deep, friendly moon voice.

If you wish to incorporate motions or use a musical instrument for accompaniment, affix the moon to a Velcro or magnet board and point to it as you lead the group in the actions or play and sing the song. You can also simply transfer the moon from one hand to the other while doing the motions.

Utilize the sections of Mother Goose Rhyme Time that work best for you and your storytime group or classroom. Experiment with new ideas and techniques. Practice ahead of time so you feel comfortable with the material and can focus on the audience rather than on trying to remember how you intended to share the rhyme.

Storytime

"The Man in the Moon" is an ideal rhyme to use as the close of a bedtime story program. Share it once or twice and then have the moon say "good night" and "good-bye" to the children.

The rhyme may also be said or sung as a group, rocking back and forth to keep a rhythm. Incorporate movements if desired. Share the rhyme several times, ending with a quiet rendition. Many different motions and actions are possible. Here are a few options:

Babies (*Sitting on caregivers' laps*)

> The Man in the Moon
> Looked out of the moon,
> (*Rock baby back and forth.*)
> Looked out of the moon and said:
> "It's time for all these children on the earth
> (*Gently tap baby's chest.*)
> To think about going to bed!"
> (*Make "shhhhh" sound with finger to lips.*)

Older Children (*Sitting or standing*)

> The Man in the Moon
> (*Arms up over head in a circle.*)
> Looked out of the moon,
> (*Hand above eyes, look one direction.*)
> Looked out of the moon and said:
> (*Other hand above eyes, look other direction.*)
> "It's time for all these children on the earth
> (*Hands out, as if patting small heads.*)
> To think about going to bed!"
> (*Rest head on hands.*)

Early Literacy Activities

Consider integrating one or several of the activities or techniques suggested below as you share the nursery rhyme. All activities should be approached in a fun and playful manner, encouraging curiosity and allowing for children's individual differences. **Note:** Be aware of children's developmental stages and focus on the activities that are appropriate for the ages and stages of your group. The suggestions provided are intended to give you a variety of ideas to work with over time. You will not incorporate all of the techniques at once. Share one rhyme several times during a single storytime, and repeat the same rhyme over several storytimes. Try different activities to highlight a different skill during each storytime.

Print Motivation (*Encourage interest in and excitement about reading and books.*)

- Say the words rhythmically and with enthusiasm, conveying your enjoyment of the rhyme.

- Repeat the rhyme several times together with the children, encouraging their own enjoyment and internalization of its stately rhythms.

- Create a voice for the Man in the Moon, and change your tone and facial expression as appropriate to the context.

Language and Vocabulary (*Introduce and explain new words or new meanings to familiar words.*)

- Use the rhyme piece to illustrate and help explain language and vocabulary. Talk

about the "Man in the Moon." Is there really a man in the moon? No, but people used to think that the moon looked like a person's face. They imagined they could see eyes *(point to the moon's eyes)* and a nose *(point to the moon's nose)* and mouth *(point to the moon's mouth)* when they looked at the moon, so they talked about the "man in the moon." Show the children a real photograph of the moon, and discuss whether or not you see shadows that make the real moon look like a face. The moon talks about "all these children on the earth"—the earth is the planet where we live, so he is talking to us!

- Talk or sing about the moon illustration: "I see the moon's nose." "I see the moon's mouth." Pause for the children to name the feature to which you are pointing: "I see the moon's _____." Expand on descriptive features of the illustrations to build vocabulary and encourage the children's awareness of and attention to details: "I see the moon's mouth. The moon's mouth is smiling."

Phonological Awareness *(Play with rhymes, practice breaking words apart and putting them back together, and listen for beginning sounds and alliteration.)*

- Play with the words and objects in the rhyme and change them. For example:

  The Man in the Moon
  Looked out of the moon,
  Looked out of the moon and said:
  "It's time for all these children on the earth,
  To sit and have a storybook read!"

- Explain that rhyming words sound the same at the end, giving examples. Try pausing just before the end of a rhyming pair and encourage the children to supply the rhyming word (such as "read" above) with the support of visual clues or context, or simply through the sounds suggested by the rhyme.

- Talk about: Who else besides children does the moon see when he looks down on the earth? Make up proclamations for the moon to say to them, such as:

  The Man in the Moon
  Looked out of the moon,
  Looked out of the moon and said:
  "It's time for all these horses on the farm,
  To come into the barn and be fed."

- Play an "oddity task" game. For example, which word does not rhyme? Earth, said, bed. *(Answer: earth.)* Which word sounds different at the beginning? Man, moon, looked. *(Answer: looked.)*

- Blend word parts in a variety of ways.

  <u>Syllables</u>: chil ... dren. What's the word? *(Children.)*

  <u>Onset sound</u>: /m/ ... an. What's the word? *(Man.)* What other words start with /m/?

  <u>Phoneme by phoneme (for older children, in primary grades)</u>: /m/-/oo/-/n/. What's the word? *(Moon.)*

- Practice segmenting or "stretching" the nursery rhyme words (for older children, in primary grades). Show the children a rubber band and stretch it out and in. As you stretch the rubber band out longer, you can see all of its parts more clearly. Explain that you can also stretch words, so that you can hear each individual sound (phoneme) in the word. Stretch the word "man": /m/-/a/-/n/. Sometimes one phoneme is represented by more than one letter, such as in the word "moon": /m/-/oo/-/n/. "Moon" contains three phonemes. Stretch other nursery rhyme words.

- Clap words: Clap once for each word in the rhyme, following the poster. Introduce variety by stomping feet or jumping once for each word.

- Clap syllables: Older children can learn to clap once for each syllable in the rhyme. Practice with one word at a time as the children begin to understand the concept. For example: The (1 clap); Man (1 clap); in (1 clap); the (1 clap); Moon (1 clap); looked (1 clap); out (1 clap); of (1 clap); the (1 clap); moon (1 clap). Introduce variety by stomping feet or jumping to the syllables.

Print Awareness *(Notice print and know how to handle books and follow the written word on a page.)*

- Point to "The Man in the Moon" poster. Say: "Our nursery rhyme is written right up here. I'll read it aloud, and then we'll say it again together." Follow the text of the rhyme with your finger as you read the poster, from left to right.

- Occasionally turn the poster upside down or sideways and see if the children detect the problem.

Narrative Skills (*Practice retelling stories or events, sequencing the order in which events happened, and adding descriptions.*)

- Talk and ask two or three open-ended questions about the rhyme, and allow the children to ask questions. Avoid asking yes/no questions unless there is a specific purpose in doing so. For example: What is the Man in the Moon telling us? How might he know it is time for us to go to bed? What are some of the clues that would tell the moon what time it is? What might the moon do during the day? (Share scientific facts, but then also concoct some imaginative ideas together as a group just for fun!) What do you think about when you look at the moon?

Letter Knowledge—Letter M (*Learn to recognize and identify letters, knowing that they have different names and sounds and that the same letter can look different.*)

- Show a large-size cutout or magnet-backed foam letter "M" and "m" (see Resources). Point to the capital "M" letters that begin the words "Man" and "Moon" in the title of your poster. Say: "Here is the letter M—a big uppercase, or capital M." Draw the capital letter "M" in the air as a group. Point to a small letter "m" on the poster within the rhyme's text. Say: "Here is also the letter m—a small, lowercase m." Draw a lowercase "m" in the air as a group. Make the /M/ sound and say: "M is for Man; M is for Moon; M is for Mouse; M is for Milk; M is for Mail; M is for Mommy; M is for Me." Encourage the audience to repeat each phrase after you. Include three or four examples.

- Demonstrate making the shapes of "M" and "m" using string or pipe cleaners.

Parent/Caregiver Connection

- Reinforce the parent/caregiver's key role in their child's early literacy development through comfortable, relaxed times together with songs, rhymes, and books. Emphasize fun and enjoyment as the goals.

- Encourage caregivers to participate during storytime and to incorporate "The Man in the Moon" at home during play and reading times. Select one of "The Man in the Moon" early literacy activities that you share together during storytime, and briefly explain how the activity supports children's early literacy development. Suggest repeating the activity at home. Try different activities to highlight different skills during each storytime.

- Share information about Dialogic, or "Hear and Say" Reading (see Resources). Encourage parents and caregivers to individually discuss the day's rhyme, its characters, and events in an open-ended way with their children, following the child's interest while affirming and expanding upon his or her answers. For example, point to the moon in "The Man in the Moon" and ask, "Who is this?" Child: "Moon." Follow up with positive affirmation, and enlarge: "Yes, it's the moon with a face. What do you see on his face?" Child: "Eyes." Expand: "Yes, he has two eyes that are open—one, two." Help the child repeat longer phrases. Ask open-ended questions such as: "What do you see in this picture?" Build on the things that catch the child's interest. This type of positive, interactive discussion around familiar rhymes and books helps improve early language development, communication, and parent/child relationships.

Take-home "The Man in the Moon"

Copy "The Man in the Moon" illustration from page 56 onto card stock and distribute. Color and cut out the moon at the end of storytime, or encourage the families to do so at home. Glue or tape the moon securely onto a wide craft stick if desired. Make a sample of the take-home version, and demonstrate singing or saying the rhyme using the small piece. (Families may also affix sticky-back magnet material to the moon for playtime use on a magnetic surface such as a cookie sheet or the refrigerator if desired. Be aware of choking hazard considerations for younger children.)

Additional Extension Ideas

Note: For all craft activities, provide materials for adult attendees as well as children. Encourage children and adults to talk together about what they are making, and to use the completed crafts to retell or act out the rhyme.

- Show the pictures from several different nursery rhyme books that illustrate "The Man in the Moon," and repeat the rhyme together with each new illustration. Talk about the differences between the various illustrations.

- Make a Man in the Moon Gets Ready for Bed craft. Use white paper plates for the moon's face, and affix paper arms and legs. Use patterned wallpaper from old wallpaper books to make him some moon pajamas!

- Make Man in the Moon masks. Cut out the centers of white paper plates and tape a paper headband to two opposite edges so the band can fit down over the children's heads. The children can look and talk through the center hole to be the Boy in the Moon or the Girl in the Moon. Consider having each child make an announcement while wearing their mask, such as "It's time for bed!" or "I'm the _____ in the Moon and it's time for bed!"

- Make the Boy/Girl in the Moon pop-up puppets from paper cups. Tape a small picture of each child's face to the end of a drinking straw and slide the other end of the straw through a hole punctured in the bottom of the paper cup. Glue or tape a picture of the moon to the outside of the cup. Pull the straw down so the child's picture is hidden inside the cup, then pop it up as you prepare to say the rhyme as a group. See page 19 in *A Pocketful of Puppets: Mother Goose* by Tamara Hunt and Nancy Renfro (Nancy Renfro Studios, 1998).

- Make a double-sided Man in the Moon stick puppet. Draw or glue features to create a funny man's face on the eating side of a heavy white paper plate. On the underside of the plate, draw a moon face. Tape a craft stick to the plate. Show the moon face first, then flip the plate around to the man's face as you say the rhyme.

- Talk about: What time does the moon go to bed and what time does it get up? Make a white paper plate "moon clock" craft with card stock hands and a metal brad fastener center so the hands may be turned. Decorate the clock with shiny star stickers and glitter.

- Talk about: Other planets in our solar system besides Earth. Make a model of the solar system using various sizes of Styrofoam balls.

- Make the shapes of "M" and "m" using string, pipe cleaners, or clay.

- Make a giant Man in the Moon character from cardboard, with a face-sized hole in the middle. The children can look through it one at a time while saying "The Man in the Moon" or some other rhyme or fact. Use the prop to segue stories, announce upcoming activities to the children, and so forth.

For example:

The Man in the Moon
Looked out of the moon,
Looked out of the moon and said:
"It's time for all these children on the earth,
To sit and have a storybook read!"

The Man in the Moon
Looked out of the moon,
Looked out of the moon and said:
"It's time for all these children on the earth,
To have a little snack and be fed!"

The Man in the Moon
Looked out of the moon,
Looked out of the moon and said:
"It's time for all these children on the earth,
To take a nap and rest their heads!"

- Sing "Mr. Moon" (adapted from the classic children's song "Mister Sun") with "The Man in the Moon" Mother Goose Rhyme Time figure. The tune for "Mister Sun" is included on the following sound recordings:
  - McGrath, Bob. *If You're Happy & You Know It ... Sing Along With Bob #1*. Bob's Kids Music, 1996, 1990.
  - Raffi. *Singable Songs for the Very Young.* Troubador Records Ltd., 1976.

  Mister Moon, moon, Mister silver moon,
  Please shine down on me.
  Oh, Mister Moon, moon, Mister silver moon,
  Hiding behind a tree.
  These little children are telling you,
  It's time for us to say good-night to you.
  Oh Mister Moon, moon, Mister silver moon,
  Please shine down on me!

- Use "The Man in the Moon" Mother Goose Rhyme Time figure as a basis for Aikendrum, the title character of the classic "Aikendrum" folk song whose head and body are constructed from a wide variety of edible and variable ingredients. Make sure "The Man in the Moon" is laminated so facial features may be safely affixed to him with bits of rolled-up masking or painter's tape. Make spaghetti hair (ivory colored yarn works well), meatball eyes (use giant pom-poms), a foamies cheese nose, and foamies or card stock pizza mouth to match children's singer Raffi's version of "Aikendrum" (available on *Singable Songs for the Very Young*, Troubador Records Ltd., 1976); or make up other options of your own. "Aikendrum" may also be presented entirely as a tell-and-draw song, where you simply draw his various body parts on a large sheet of paper as the audience calls them out—such as "His hands were made of ... broccoli," and so forth. Be creative and have fun! Extend "Aikendrum" further as a craft project. Use paper plates for the moon face, and attach paper arms and legs. Supply medium brown pom-poms, various colored foamies and felt pieces, paper, and yarn for the children to create Aikendrum's face and body.

"Aikendrum"

There was a man lived in the moon,
In the moon, in the moon.
There was a man lived in the moon,
And his name was Aikendrum.

Chorus:
And he played upon a ladle,
A ladle, a ladle.
He played upon a ladle,
And his name was Aikendrum.

And his hair was made of spaghetti,
Spaghetti, spaghetti.
His hair was made of spaghetti,
And his name was Aikendrum.

And his eyes were made of meatballs,
Meatballs, meatballs.
His eyes were made of meatballs,
And his name was Aikendrum.

Chorus

And his nose was made of cheese,
Cheese, cheese.
His nose was made of cheese,
And his name was Aikendrum.

And his mouth was made of pizza,
Pizza, pizza.
His mouth was made of pizza,
And his name was Aikendrum.

Chorus

There was a man lived in the moon,
In the moon, in the moon.
There was a man lived in the moon,
And his name was Aikendrum.

The Man in the Moon

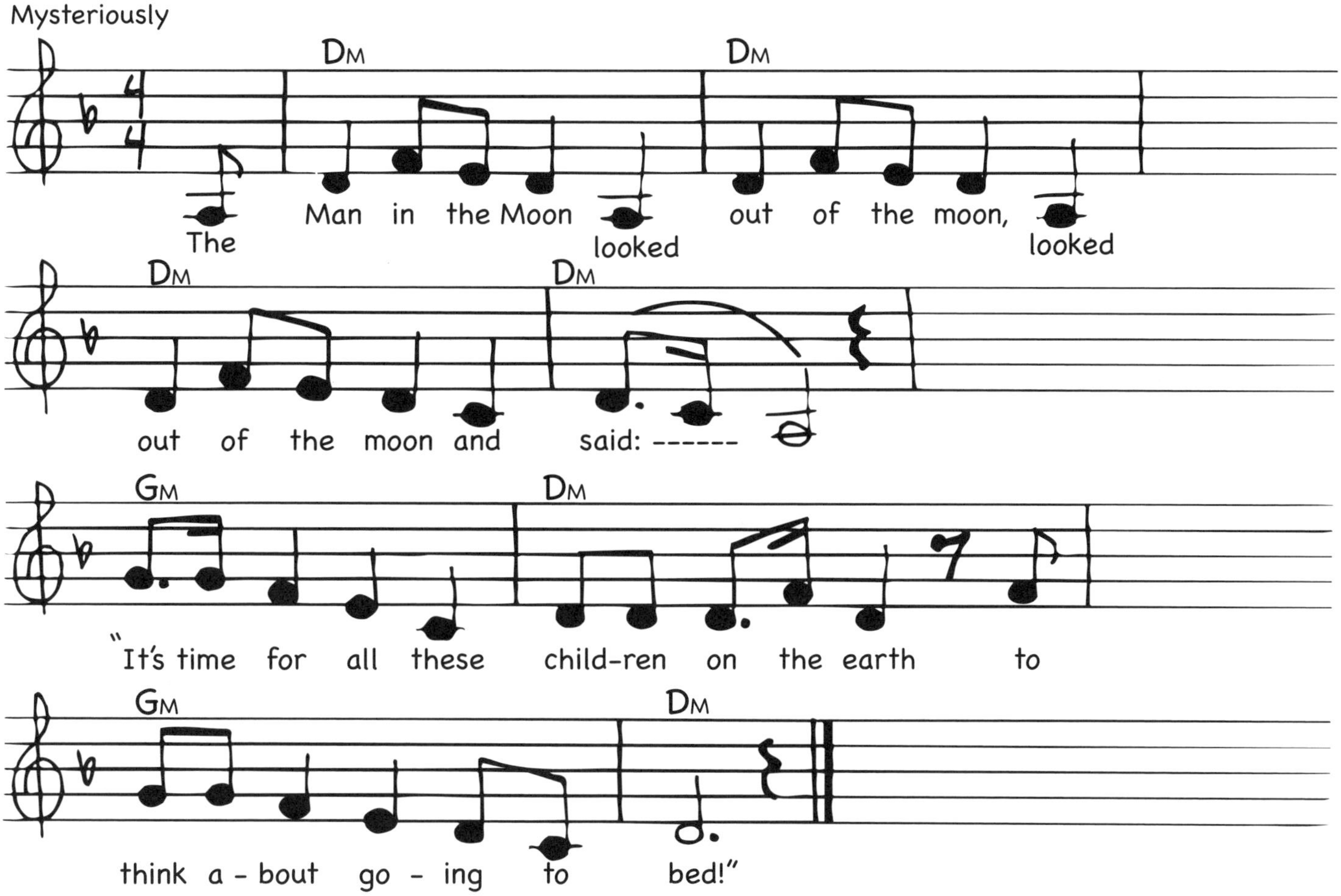
Mysteriously
Dm Dm
The Man in the Moon looked out of the moon, looked
Dm Dm
out of the moon and said: ------
Gm Dm
"It's time for all these child-ren on the earth to
Gm Dm
think a - bout go - ing to bed!"

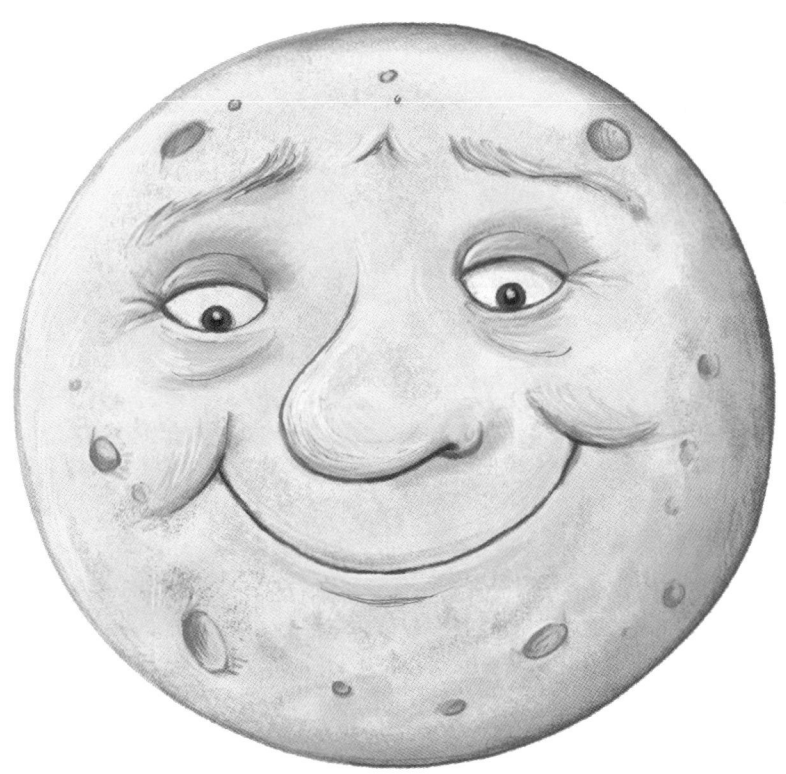

Take-home The Man in the Moon

The Man in the Moon
Looked out of the moon,
Looked out of the moon and said:
"It's time for all these children on the earth
To think about going to bed!"

There Was an Old Woman Tossed Up in a Basket

> There was an old woman tossed up in a basket,
> Seventeen times as high as the moon.
> Where she was going I couldn't but ask it,
> For in her hand she carried a broom.
>
> "Old woman, old woman, old woman," said I,
> "Where are you going to up so high?"
> "To brush the cobwebs off the sky!"
> "May I go with you?"
> "Aye, by-and-by."

Variants

Several minor variants include the old woman being "toss'd in a blanket" instead of a basket, the use of "quoth I" instead of "said I," and sweeping the cobwebs from the sky instead of brushing them. Another alternate version follows:

> There was an old woman tossed up in a basket
> Seventeen times as high as the moon;
> But where she was going no mortal could tell,
> For under her arm she carried a broom.
>
> "Old woman, old woman, old woman," said I,
> "Whither, oh whither, oh whither so high?"
> "To sweep the cobwebs from the sky;
> And I'll be with you by-and-by."

History

As with many nursery rhymes, scholars disagree about the song's origins. Some say it refers to King James II, while others point to the editor's preface to *Mother Goose's Melody* (c. 1765), which identifies the old woman as King Henry V (1387–1422) of England. The words were supposedly written by political opponents of Henry's highly unpopular but unexpectedly successful war against France, and the tune is that of the famous Irish song "Lilliburlero."

In various historical versions, the old woman is tossed 10, 19, 50, 70, and even 99 times as high as the moon. The original words were probably "tossed up in a blanket / Ninety-nine times as high as the moon."

Musical Notation

See musical notation on page 63.

Preparing and Using the Mother Goose Rhyme Time Pieces

"There Was an Old Woman Tossed Up in a Basket" pieces:

- Old woman with broom in large basket
- Large moon with face (this moon will also be used for "Hey Diddle Diddle" and "The Man in the Moon")
- "There Was an Old Woman Tossed Up in a Basket" poster

The moon may be used exactly as it is and held in your hand, or it may be glued or taped securely to a thick dowel rod or paint stirrer to create a giant moon stick puppet. If you choose to leave the moon as it is, you may wish to display it high (but still within your reach) on a wall or hang it from the ceiling with a paper clip attached to fishing line.

The sky's cobwebs may be entirely imaginary, or consider hanging fake Halloween spider web gossamer from the ceiling and from the moon for the old woman to brush with her broom.

Before sharing the rhyme, place the poster on an easel so the audience can see it clearly. Hold the moon high up in one hand and with the other hand make a tossing movement with the old woman in her basket. Move her up higher than the moon as you sing or say "seventeen times as high as the moon." Look up at the old woman as you ask her where she is going, and make her bob about and look down at you as she replies to your question. Make gentle swaying, brushing movements with the old woman in her basket as she sweeps the sky.

If you wish to incorporate motions or use a musical instrument for accompaniment, affix the pieces to a Velcro or magnet board and point to them as you lead the group in the actions or play and sing the song.

Utilize the sections of Mother Goose Rhyme Time that work best for you and your storytime group or classroom. Experiment with new ideas and techniques. Practice ahead of time so you feel comfortable with the material and can focus on the audience rather than on trying to remember how you intended to share the rhyme.

Storytime

The rhyme may be said or sung as a group, rocking back and forth to keep a gentle rhythm. Incorporate actions if desired. Share the rhyme several times. Many different motions are possible. Here are a few options:

Babies *(Sitting on caregivers' laps)*

There was an old woman tossed up in a basket,
(Lift baby in the air on "up.")
Seventeen times as high as the moon.
(Sway baby in the air, then down.)
Where she was going I couldn't but ask it,
(Rock baby.)
For in her hand she carried a broom.
(Make sweeping gesture with fingers.)

"Old woman, old woman, old woman," said I,
(Rock baby.)
"Where are you going to up so high?"
(Lift baby in the air on "up.")
"To brush the cobwebs off the sky!"
(Brush/tickle baby gently with fingers.)
"May I go with you?"
(Rock baby.)
"Aye, by-and-by."

Older Children *(Sitting or standing)*

There was an old woman tossed up in a basket,
(Arms up.)
Seventeen times as high as the moon.
(Wave arms back and forth over head, while rocking back and forth.)
Where she was going I couldn't but ask it,
For in her hand she carried a broom.

"Old woman, old woman, old woman," said I,
(Hands to mouth as if calling, point to self on "I.")
"Where are you going to up so high?"
(Hands to mouth as if calling.)
"To brush the cobwebs off the sky!"
(Pretend to sweep the air.)
"May I go with you?"
(Hands out questioningly.)
"Aye, by-and-by."
(Nod head.)

Early Literacy Activities

Consider integrating one or several of the activities or techniques suggested below as you share the nursery rhyme. All activities should be approached in a fun and playful manner, encouraging curiosity and allowing for children's individual differences. **Note:** Be aware of children's developmental stages and focus on the activities that are appropriate for the ages and stages of your group. The suggestions provided are intended to give you a variety of ideas to work with over time. You will not incorporate all of the techniques at once. Share one rhyme several times during a single storytime, and repeat the same rhyme over several storytimes. Try different activities to highlight a different skill during each storytime.

Print Motivation *(Encourage interest in and excitement about reading and books.)*

- Say the words rhythmically and with enthusiasm, conveying your enjoyment of the rhyme.

- Repeat the rhyme several times together with the children, encouraging their own enjoyment and internalization of its gentle rhythms.

- Create voices for the characters, and change your tone and facial expression as appropriate to the context.

Language and Vocabulary *(Introduce and explain new words or new meanings to familiar words.)*

- Use the rhyme pieces to illustrate and help explain language and vocabulary. Pause momentarily as you point to familiar objects for the children to supply the name or word if they know it. Say: "The old woman *(point to the old woman)* in our rhyme was in a basket *(point to basket)*. Her basket was tossed, or gently thrown, up into the sky. It went up really high, because it went 'seventeen times as high as the moon' *(point to the moon)*. That is really far away! The old woman was carrying a broom *(point to broom)* in her hand. She is going to brush the cobwebs off the sky—cobwebs are spider webs. The old woman says we can go with her eventually—she says 'Aye,' which means 'yes,' and 'by-and-by,' which means not right now but a little bit later."

- Talk or sing about the illustrations: "I see a broom." "I see the moon." Pause for the children to name the object to which you are pointing: "I see a _____." Expand on descriptive features of the illustrations to build vocabulary and encourage the children's awareness of and attention to details: "I see a woman. A woman wearing a white hat and sitting in a basket."

Phonological Awareness *(Play with rhymes, practice breaking words apart and putting them back together, and listen for beginning sounds and alliteration.)*

- Explain that rhyming words sound the same at the end. "Basket" and "ask it" sound alike, as do "I," "high," "sky," and "by." Say the rhyme, listening for the rhyming pairs.

- Play an "oddity task" game. For example, which word does not rhyme? Tossed, high, sky. *(Answer: tossed.)* Which word sounds different at the beginning? Was, basket, woman. *(Answer: basket.)*

- Blend word parts in a variety of ways.

  <u>Syllables:</u> bas ... ket. What's the word? *(Basket.)*

  <u>Onset sound:</u> /h/ ... and. What's the word? *(Hand.)* What other words start with /h/?

  <u>Phoneme by phoneme (for older children, in primary grades):</u> /b/-/r/-/oo/-/m/. What's the word? *(Broom.)*

- Practice segmenting or "stretching" the nursery rhyme words (for older children, in primary grades). Show the children a rubber band and stretch it out and in. As you stretch the rubber band out longer, you can see all of its parts more clearly. Explain that you can also stretch words, so that you can hear each individual sound (phoneme) in the word. Stretch the word "old": /o/-/l/-/d/. Sometimes one phoneme is represented by more than one letter, such as in the word "broom": /b/-/r/-/oo/-/m/. "Broom" contains four phonemes. Stretch other nursery rhyme words.

- Clap words: Clap once for each word in the rhyme, following the poster. Introduce variety by stomping feet or jumping once for each word.

- Clap syllables: Older children can learn to clap once for each syllable in the rhyme. Practice with one word at a time as the children begin to understand the concept. For example: There (1 clap); was (1 clap); an (1 clap); old (1 clap); wom-an (2 claps); tossed (1 clap); up (1 clap); in (1 clap); a (1 clap); bas-ket (2 claps). Introduce variety by stomping feet or jumping to the syllables.

Print Awareness *(Notice print and know how to handle books and follow the written word on a page.)*

- Point to the "There Was an Old Woman Tossed Up in a Basket" poster. Say: "Our nursery rhyme is written right up here. I'll read it aloud, and then we'll say it again together." Follow the text of the rhyme with your finger as you read the poster, from left to right.

- Occasionally turn the poster upside down or sideways and see if the children detect the problem.

Narrative Skills *(Practice retelling stories or events, sequencing the order in which events happened, and adding descriptions.)*

- Talk and ask two or three open-ended questions about the rhyme and the objects and characters in it, and allow the children to ask questions. Avoid asking yes/no questions unless there is a specific purpose in doing so. Qualify questions by including the phrase "do you think," as in "Why do you think …?" or "What do you think …?" This type of question does not have a "right" answer that children are afraid they will get wrong. For example: If the old woman is going up into outer space "seventeen times as high as the moon," what do you think she needs to get ready? What do you think she should wear? How do you think she will get the basket to go up in the air? What do you think she should bring to eat and drink?

- How far is "seventeen times as high as the moon"? It would be more than four million miles! Since it would take too long to count to four million, count to seventeen as a group instead.

- Talk about: The old woman says she is going to brush the "cobwebs" off the sky. What makes cobwebs? Do you think spiders really live in outer space and on the moon? If there were outer space spiders, what would they look like? What do you think the spiders would need to wear?

- If you have a small enough group and adequate time, act out "There Was an Old Woman Tossed Up in a Basket" with creative dramatics. Use a large plastic laundry basket or cardboard box for the old woman's basket (avoid wicker as it can have sharp points). Have the children take turns sitting on the floor in the basket as the "old woman" or "old man." Give the child in the basket a paper broom (see Additional Extension Ideas on page 61) or feather duster with which to brush (gently, and no faces!), and have the other children be the stars and moon. Have the stars and moon circle past the child in the basket and each be lightly brushed. Have the children take turns asking to ride in the basket with the old woman/man.

Letter Knowledge—Letter W *(Learn to recognize and identify letters, knowing that they have different names and sounds and that the same letter can look different.)*

- Show a large-size cutout or magnet-backed foam letter "W" and "w" (see Resources). Point to the capital "W" letters that begin the words "Was" and "Woman" in the title of your poster. Say: "Here is the letter W—a big uppercase, or capital W." Draw the capital letter "W" in the air as a group. Point to a small letter "w" on the poster within the rhyme's text. Say: "Here is also the letter w—a small, lowercase w." Draw a lowercase "w" in the air as a group. Make the /W/ sound and say: "W is for Was; W is for Woman; W is for Water; W is for Window; W is for Wash; W is for Worm; W is for Wait; W is for Want; W is for Wind." Encourage the audience to repeat each phrase after you. Include three or four examples.

- Demonstrate making the shapes of "W" and "w" using string or pipe cleaners.

Parent/Caregiver Connection

- Reinforce the parent/caregiver's key role in their child's early literacy development through comfortable, relaxed times together with songs, rhymes, and books. Emphasize fun and enjoyment as the goals.

- Encourage caregivers to participate during storytime and to incorporate "There Was an Old Woman Tossed Up in a Basket" at home during play and reading times. Select one of the "Old Woman Tossed Up in a Basket" early literacy activities that you share together during storytime, and briefly explain how the activity supports children's early literacy development. Suggest repeating the activity at home. Try different activities to highlight different skills during each storytime.

- Share information about Dialogic, or "Hear and Say" Reading (see Resources). Encourage parents and caregivers to individually discuss the day's rhyme, its characters, and events in an open-ended way with their children, following the child's interest while affirming and expanding upon their answers. For example, point to the old woman in "There Was an Old Woman Tossed Up in a Basket" and ask, "Who is this?" Child: "Lady." Follow up with positive affirmation, and enlarge: "Yes, it's a lady, or a woman sitting in a basket. What do you notice about the lady?" Child: "Broom." Expand: "Yes, she is holding a broom in her hand." Help the child repeat longer phrases. Ask open-ended questions such as: "What do you see in this picture?" Build on the things that catch the child's interest. This type of positive, interactive discussion around familiar rhymes and books helps improve early language development, communication, and parent/child relationships.

Take-home "There Was an Old Woman Tossed Up in a Basket"

Copy the "There Was an Old Woman Tossed Up in a Basket" illustrations from pages 64 and 65 onto card stock and distribute. Color and cut out the pieces at the end of storytime, or encourage the families to do so at home. Glue or tape the moon securely onto a wide craft stick if desired. Make a sample of the take-home version, and demonstrate singing or saying the rhyme using the small pieces. (Families may affix sticky-back magnet material to pieces for playtime use on a magnetic surface such as a cookie sheet or the refrigerator if desired. Be aware of choking hazard considerations for younger children.)

Additional Extension Ideas

Note: For all craft activities, provide materials for adult attendees as well as children. Encourage children and adults to talk together about what they are making, and to use the completed crafts to retell or act out the rhyme.

- Show the pictures from several different nursery rhyme books that illustrate "There Was an Old Woman Tossed Up in a Basket," and repeat the rhyme together with each new illustration. Talk about the differences between the various illustrations.

- Make an Old Woman Travels Into Outer Space craft. Give each child a deep paper bowl or large-size beverage cup for a "basket." Have the children draw the old woman with her broom, a space suit, food, a teddy bear, and other things she will need to bring. Cut the pictures out and put them in the "baskets." Decorate the "baskets" with rockets, stars, and so forth as desired for outer space travel. Sing or say the rhyme as a group while each child manipulates his or her own basket.

- Make Space Spiders drawings or a craft with pom-poms, pipe cleaners, yarn, and felt. Use to retell or act out the rhyme.

- Look at pictures of actual spider webs. What would outer space spider webs look like? Would they have pictures of stars and the moon in them? What kind of bugs would space spider webs catch? Outline some imaginary space webs with glitter glue on paper and let them dry completely. Make space spiders and space bugs from paper, felt, or pom-poms, and glue them to the webs.

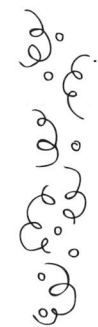

- Make soft paper brooms from paper strips bound tightly to the bottom of a craft or popsicle stick with yarn. Use to retell or act out the rhyme.
- Make large star cutouts to hang from the ceiling on fishing line. Glue plastic spiders and Halloween spider web gossamer to them.
- Make a Twinkle Star Finger Puppet craft from an unwanted shiny CD disk! Complete instructions are included in the book *Crafts from your Favorite Children's Songs* by Kathy Ross (Millbrook Press, 2001).
- Make the shapes of "W" and "w" using string, pipe cleaners, or clay.

There Was an Old Woman Tossed Up in a Basket

Take-home There Was an Old Woman Tossed Up in a Basket

There was an old woman tossed up in a basket,
Seventeen times as high as the moon.
Where she was going I couldn't but ask it,
For in her hand she carried a broom.

"Old woman, old woman, old woman," said I,
"Where are you going to up so high?"
"To brush the cobwebs off the sky!"
"May I go with you?"
"Aye, by-and-by."

Bibliographies and Resources

Mother Goose Collections to Share and Recommend

Alderson, Brian (sel.). *Cakes and Custard.* William Morrow & Co., 1975, 1974.

Crews, Nina. *The Neighborhood Mother Goose.* Greenwillow Books, 2004.

dePaola, Tomie. *Tomie dePaola's Mother Goose.* Putnam, 1985.

Engelbreit, Mary. *Mary Engelbreit's Mother Goose: One Hundred Best-Loved Verses.* HarperCollins, 2005.

Foreman, Michael. *Michael Foreman's Mother Goose.* Harcourt, 1991.

Hoberman, Mary Ann. *You Read to Me, I'll Read to You: Very Short Mother Goose Tales to Read Together.* Little, Brown and Company, 2005.

Kubler, Annie, illus. *Pat-a-Cake!: Nursery Rhymes.* Child's Play, 2005. (Board book)

Kubler, Annie, illus. *Peek-a-Boo!: Nursery Games.* Child's Play, 2005. (Board book)

Kubler, Annie, illus. *See-Saw! Nursery Songs.* Child's Play, 2005. (Board book)

Lansky, Bruce. *Mary Had a Little Jam and Other Silly Rhymes.* Meadowbrook Press, 2004. Reprint of *The New Adventures of Mother Goose: Gentle Rhymes for Happy Times* (1993).

Lobel, Arnold. *Arnold Lobel's Book of Mother Goose.* Knopf, 1997. Reprint of *The Random House Book of Mother Goose* (1986).

Long, Sylvia. *Sylvia Long's Mother Goose.* Chronicle Books, 1999.

Opie, Iona, ed. Illus. by Rosemary Wells. *My Very First Mother Goose.* Candlewick Press, 1996.

Opie, Iona, ed. Illus. by Rosemary Wells. *Here Comes Mother Goose.* Candlewick Press, 1999.

Scarry, Richard. *Richard Scarry's Best Mother Goose Ever.* Western Publishing Co., 1970, 1964.

Smith, Jessie Willcox. *The Jessie Willcox Smith Mother Goose.* Derrydale Books, 1986.

Wright, Blanche Fisher, illus. *The Real Mother Goose.* Checkerboard Press, 1944, 1916.

Yaccarino, Dan, illus. *Dan Yaccarino's Mother Goose.* Random House, 2004.

History of Nursery Rhymes

Baring-Gould, William S., and Cecil Baring-Gould. *The Annotated Mother Goose.* Crown Publishers, 1962.

Christensen, James C. *Rhymes & Reasons: An Annotated Collection of Mother Goose Rhymes.* The Greenwich Workshop Press, 1977.

Delamar, Gloria T. *Mother Goose: From Nursery to Literature.* McFarland, 1987.

Montgomery, Michael G., and Wayne Montgomery. *Over the Candlestick: Classic Nursery Rhymes and the Real Stories Behind Them.* Peachtree Publishers, 2002.

Opie, Iona and Peter, eds. *The Oxford Dictionary of Nursery Rhymes.* Clarendon Press, 1951.

Roberts, Chris. *Heavy Words Lightly Thrown: The Reason Behind the Rhyme.* Gotham Books, 2005.

Stevens, Albert Mason. *The Nursery Rhyme: Remnant of Popular Protest.* Coronado Press, 1968.

Thomas, K. E. *The Real Personages of Mother Goose.* Lothrop, Lee & Shepard, 1930.

Mother Goose Crafts

Cressy, Judith. *What Can You Do with a Paper Bag? Hats, Wigs, Masks, Crowns, Helmets, and Headdresses.* Chronicle Books, 2001.

Renfro, Nancy, and Tamara Hunt. *A Pocketful of Puppets: Mother Goose.* Nancy Renfro Studios, 1982.

Ross, Kathy. *Crafts From Your Favorite Children's Songs.* Millbrook Press, 2001.

Ross, Kathy. *Crafts From Your Favorite Nursery Rhymes.* Millbrook Press, 2002.

Ross, Kathy. *Crafts to Make in the Spring.* Millbrook Press, 1998.

Mother Goose Songbooks

Barratt, Carol. *The Mother Goose Songbook: Nursery Rhymes to Play and Sing.* Arranged for the piano by Carol Barratt. Derrydale Books, 1984.

Beall, Pamela Conn, and Susan Hagen Nipp. *Wee Sing Nursery Rhymes & Lullabies.* Price Stern Sloan, 2005, 2002, 1985.

Buck, Sir Percy. *The Oxford Nursery Song Book.* 3d ed. Oxford University Press, 1984, 1961, 1933.

Crane, Walter. *The Baby's Bouquet.* Robert Frederick Ltd., 1994. (First published in 1877.)

Crane, Walter. *The Baby's Opera.* Simon & Schuster, 1981. (First published in 1879.)

Larrick, Nancy, comp. *Songs from Mother Goose: With the Traditional Melody for Each.* Harper & Row, 1989.

Orth, L. E. *Sixty Songs from Mother Goose.* Set to music by L. E. Orth. Oliver Ditson Company, 1906.

Rey, H. A. *Humpty Dumpty: And Other Mother Goose Songs.* HarperFestival, 1995.

Sharon, Lois & Bram's Mother Goose. Little, Brown and Company, 1985.

Yolen, Jane. *Jane Yolen's Mother Goose Songbook.* Boyds Mills Press, 1992.

Yolen, Jane, ed. *This Little Piggy: And Other Rhymes to Sing and Play.* [Music CD included.] Candlewick Press, 2005.

Sound Recordings

Beall, Pamela Conn, and Susan Hagen Nipp. *Wee Sing Nursery Rhymes & Lullabies.* Price Stern Sloan, 2005, 2002, 1985.

The Countdown Kids. *Mommy and Me: Mary Had a Little Lamb.* Mommy and Me Enterprises, 1998.

The Countdown Kids. *Mommy and Me: Old MacDonald Had a Farm.* Mommy and Me Enterprises, 1998.

The Countdown Kids. *Mommy and Me: Rock-a-bye Baby.* Mommy and Me Enterprises, 1998.

The Countdown Kids. *Mommy and Me: Twinkle Twinkle Little Star.* Mommy and Me Enterprises, 1998.

Feldman, Jean. *Nursery Rhymes and Good Ol' Times with Dr. Jean.* Jean Feldman, 2002.

Hegner, Priscilla A. *Baby Games (6 Weeks - 1 Year).* Kimbo Educational, 1987.

Hegner, Priscilla, and Rose Grasselli. *Diaper Gym: Fun Activities for Babies on the Move.* Kimbo Educational, 1985.

Hegner, Priscilla. *Teach a Toddler: Playful Songs for Learning.* Kimbo Educational, 1985.

Jenkins, Ella. *Early, Early Childhood Songs.* Smithsonian Folkways Recordings, 1990.

Jenkins, Ella. *Nursery Rhymes: Rhyming and Remembering.* Smithsonian Folkways Recordings, 1974.

McGrath, Bob. *If You're Happy & You Know It ... Sing Along with Bob #1.* Bob's Kids Music, 1996, 1990.

McGrath, Bob, and Katharine Smithrim. *The Baby Record.* Bob's Kids Music, 2000.

McGrath, Bob, and Katharine Smithrim. *Songs & Games For Toddlers.* Bob's Kids Music, 2000.

Palmer, Hap. *Early Childhood Classics: Old Favorites With A New Twist.* Hap-Pal Music, Inc., 2000.

Palmer, Hap. *Hap Palmer Sings Classic Nursery Rhymes.* Educational Activities, Inc., 2003; Hap-Pal Music, Inc., 1991.

Raffi. *Singable Songs for the Very Young.* Troubador Records Ltd., 1976.

Sharon, Lois & Bram. *Mainly Mother Goose: Songs and Rhymes For Merry Young Souls.* Elephant Records, 1984.

Snee, Richard. *Mother Goose Rocks! Volume 1.* Boffomedia, Inc., 2000.

Sunseri, Mary Lee. *Mother Goose Melodies: Four & Twenty Olde Songs for Young Children.* Piper Grove, 2003.

Spanish Language Resources

Ada, Alma Flor, and F. Isabel Campoy. *Mama Goose: A Latino Nursery Treasury; Un Tesoro De Rimas Infantiles.* Illus. by Maribel Suarez. English editing by Tracy Hefferman. Hyperion, 2004.

Ada, Alma Flor, and F. Isabel Campoy, sel. *¡Pio Peep!: Traditional Spanish Nursery Rhymes.* English adapt. by Alice Schertle. Illus. by Vivi Escriva. HarperCollins, 2003. (Book and CD set: Rayo, 2006.)

Carlson, Ann, and Mary Carlson, illus. *Flannelboard Stories for Infants and Toddlers,* Bilingual Edition (Spanish-English). American Library Assn., 2005.

Hall, Nancy Abraham, and Jill Syverson-Stork, sel. and adapt. *Los Pollitos Dicen: Juegos, Rimas y Canciones Infantiles de Países de Habla Hispana; The Baby Chicks Sing: Traditional Games, Nursery Rhymes, and Lullabies from Spanish-Speaking Countries.* Illus. by Kay Chorao. Little, Brown and Company, 1994.

Orozco, Jose-Luis, sel., arr., and transl. *De Colores: and Other Latin-American Folk Songs for Children.* Illus. by Elisa Kleven. Dutton, 1994.

Orozco, Jose-Luis. *Jose-Luis Orozco Canta De Colores* [sound recording]. Arcoiris Records, 1996.

Orozco, Jose-Luis, sel., arr., and transl. *Diez Deditos; Ten Little Fingers & Other Play Rhymes and Action Songs from Latin America.* Illus. by Elisa Kleven. Dutton, 1997.

Orozco, Jose-Luis. *Diez Deditos* [sound recording]. Arcoiris Records, 1997.

Orozco, Jose-Luis. *Rin, Rin, Rin; Do, Re, Mi.* Illus. by David Diaz. Scholastic, 2005.

Orozco, Jose-Luis. *Rin, Rin, Rin; Do, Re, Mi* [sound recording]. Arcoiris Records, 2005.

See Jose-Luis Orozco's Web site at www.joseluisorozco.com for the following sound recordings and more:

> Orozco, Jose-Luis. *Lirica Infantil volume #1: Latin American Children's Songs, Games and Rhymes.* Arcoiris Records.
>
> Orozco, Jose-Luis. *Lirica Infantil volume #2: Latin American Children's Songs, Games and Rhymes.* Arcoiris Records.
>
> Orozco, Jose-Luis. *Lirica Infantil volume #3: Latin American Children's Songs, Games and Rhymes.* Arcoiris Records.

Where to Buy Sound Recordings

Arcoiris Records (Jose-Luis Orozco)
P.O. Box 461900
Los Angeles, CA 90046
888.354.7373 phone / 310.659.4144 fax
www.joseluisorozco.com

Educational Record Center
3233 Burnt Mill Drive, Suite 100
Wilmington, NC 28403-2698
888.372.4543 phone / 888.438.1637 fax
www.erckids.com

Kimbo Educational
P.O. Box 477 J
Long Branch, NJ 07740
800.631.2187 phone / 732.870.3340 fax
www.Kimboed.com

Music for Little People
P.O. Box 1460
Redway, CA 95560-1460
707.923.3991 phone / 800.409.2457 phone
www.musicforlittlepeople.com

Where to Buy Alphabet Letters

Childcraft Education Corp.
P. O. Box 3239
Lancaster, PA 17604
800.631.5652 phone / 888.532.4453 fax
www.childcraft.com
(Jumbo 4.7" high UPPERCASE Letters, item #5G358374; Jumbo 4.3" high LOWERCASE Letters, item #5G358382)

Constructive Playthings
13201 Arrington Road
Grandview, MO 64030-1117
800.448.4115 phone / 816.761.9295 fax
www.cptoys.com
(Giant 4.75" Magnetic Foam UPPERCASE Letters, item #EDL-776; Giant 4.75" Magnetic Foam LOWERCASE Letters, item #EDL-617)
(Jumbo 7.5" Foam UPPERCASE Letters, item #EDL-170; Jumbo 7.25" Foam LOWERCASE Letters, item #EDL-171)

Highsmith Inc.
W5527 State Road 106
P.O. Box 800
Fort Atkinson, WI 53538-0800
800.558.2110 phone / 800.835.2329 fax
www.highsmith.com
(Durafoam Letters—6", 8", 10", and 12" high)

Lakeshore Learning Materials
2695 E. Dominguez Street
Carson, CA 90895
800.778.4456 phone / 800.537.5403 fax
www.lakeshorelearning.com
(Jumbo 5" Magnetic Letters—UPPERCASE, item #RR932; Jumbo 5" Magnetic Letters—LOWERCASE, item #RR933)

Storybook and Sound Recording Titles Listed in *Mother Goose Rhyme Time: Night*

Brown, Margaret Wise. *Goodnight Moon*. Pictures by Clement Hurd. Harper and Row, 1947; Scholastic, 1975 (Big Book edition ISBN 0-590-73302-8).

Hoberman, Mary Ann. *You Read to Me, I'll Read to You: Very Short Mother Goose Tales to Read Together*. Little, Brown and Company, 2005.

Kent, Jack. *Mrs. Mooley*. Golden Books, 2002, 1973.

McGrath, Bob. *If You're Happy & You Know It ... Sing Along with Bob #1*. Bob's Kids Music, 1996, 1990.

Murphy, Stuart. *A Pair of Socks*. HarperCollins, 1996.

Raffi. *Singable Songs for the Very Young*. Troubador Records Ltd., 1976.

Speed, Toby. *Two Cool Cows*. Putnam, 1995.

Stevens, Janet, and Susan Stevens Crummel. *And the Dish Ran Away with the Spoon*. Harcourt, 2001.

Mother Goose and Early Literacy Programming Books, Articles, and Video/DVDs

Briggs, Diane. *Toddler Storytime Programs*. Scarecrow Press, 1993.

Brown, Marc, coll. and illus. *Finger Rhymes*. Dutton, 1980.

Brown, Marc, coll. and illus. *Hand Rhymes*. Dutton, 1985.

Brown, Marc, coll. and illus. *Play Rhymes*. Dutton, 1987.

Butler, Dorothy. *Babies Need Books*. Atheneum, 1980.

Clow-Martin, Elaine. *Baby Games: The Joyful Guide to Child's Play from Birth to Three Years*. Rev. ed. Fitzhenry & Whiteside Ltd., 2003, Running Press, 1988.

Cobb, Jane. *I'm a Little Teapot! Presenting Preschool Storytime*. 2d ed. Black Sheep Pr., 1996.

Cobb, Jane. *What'll I Do with the Baby-oh? Nursery Rhymes, Songs and Stories for Babies*. Black Sheep Pr., 2006.

Cole, Joanna, and Stephanie Calmenson. *The Eentsy, Weentsy Spider; Fingerplays and Action Rhymes*. William Morrow, 1991.

Cole, Joanna, and Stephanie Calmenson. *Pat-A-Cake and Other Play Rhymes*. HarperCollins, 1992.

Davis, Robin Works. *Toddle On Over: Developing Infant & Toddler Literature Programs*. Alleyside Press, 1998.

De Salvo, Nancy. *Beginning with Books: Library Programming for Infants, Toddlers, and Preschoolers.* Library Professional Publications, 1993.

Diamant-Cohen, Betsy. "Mother Goose on the Loose: Applying Brain Research to Early Childhood Programs in the Public Library." *Public Libraries,* 43.1 (2004): 41–45.

Diamant-Cohen, Betsy, Ellen Riordan, and Regina Wade. "Make Way for Dendrites: How Brain Research Can Impact Children's Programming." *Children & Libraries,* 2.1 (2004): 12–20.

Diamant-Cohen, Betsy. *Mother Goose on the Loose.* Neal Schuman, 2006.

Ernst, Linda L. *Lapsit Services for the Very Young: A How-To-Do-It Manual.* Neal Schuman, 1995.

Ernst, Linda L. *Lapsit Services for the Very Young II: A How-To-Do-It Manual.* Neal Schuman, 2001.

Fehrenbach, Laurie A., and David P. Hurford, Carolyn R. Fehrenbach, and Rebecca Groves. "Developing the Emergent Literacy of Preschool Children through a Library Outreach Program." *Journal of Youth Services in Libraries,* 12:1 (1998): 40–1.

Ghoting, Saroj Nadkarni, and Pamela Martin-Diaz. *Early Literacy Storytimes @ Your Library: Partnering with Caregivers for Success.* American Library Assn., 2006.

Greene, Ellin. *Books, Babies, and Libraries.* American Library Assn., 1991.

Herb, Steve. "Building Blocks for Literacy: What Current Research Shows." *School Library Journal,* 43.7 (1997): 23.

Huebner, Colleen E. *Hear and Say Reading* [VHS or DVD]. Rotary Club of Bainbridge Island, 2001. (www.bainbridgeislandrotary.org)

Jeffery, Debby Ann. *Literate Beginnings: Programs for Babies and Toddlers.* American Library Assn., 1995.

Jeffery, Debby, and Ellen Mahoney. "Sitting Pretty: Infants, Toddlers, & Lapsits." *School Library Journal,* 35.8 (1989): 37–9.

Marino, Jane. "B Is for Baby, B Is for Books." *School Library Journal,* 43.3 (1997): 110–11.

Marino, Jane. *Babies in the Library!* Scarecrow Press, 2003.

Marino, Jane, and Dorothy F. Houlihan. *Mother Goose Time: Library Programs for Babies and Their Caregivers.* H. W., Wilson, 1992.

McGuiness, Diane. *Growing a Reader from Birth: Your Child's Path from Language to Literacy.* W. W. Norton & Co., 2004.

Nespeca, Sue McLeaf. "Bringing Up Baby." *School Library Journal,* 45, no. 11 (November 1999): 48-52.

Nespeca, Sue McLeaf. *Library Programming for Families with Young Children: A How-to-Do-It Manual.* Neal Schuman, 1994.

Neuman, Susan B. ed., et al. *Access for All: Closing the Book Gap for Children in Early Education.* International Reading Association, 2001.

Newcome, Zita. *Head, Shoulders, Knees, and Toes; and Other Action Rhymes.* Candlewick Press, 2002.

Nichols, Judy. *Storytimes for Two-Year-Olds.* 2d ed. American Library Assn., 1998.

Silberg, Jackie, and Pam Schiller, compilers. *The Complete Book of Rhymes, Songs, Poems, Fingerplays and Chants.* Gryphon House, 2002.

Walter, Virginia A. *Output Measures for Public Library Service to Children: A Manual of Standardized Procedures.* American Library Assn., 1992.

Wilner, Isabel, sel. *The Baby's Game Book.* Illus. by Sam Williams. Greenwillow Books, 2000.

Winkel, Lois, and Sue Kimmel. *Mother Goose Comes First: An Annotated Guide to the Best Books and Recordings for Your Preschool Child.* Henry Holt & Company, 1990.

Mother Goose Programming and Early Literacy Web Connections

America Reads Challenge
www.ed.gov/inits/americareads/index.html

Association of Library Service to Children: Born to Read: How to Raise a Reader
www.ala.org/ala/alsc/alscresources/bornto read/bornread.htm

Champaign Public Library (IL): Just for Kids: Mother Goose
www.champaign.org/kids/mgoose_tips.html

Children of the Code
www.childrenofthecode.org

Early Literacy and Brain Development Resources (Saroj Ghoting)
www.earlylit.net/earlylit/bibliography.html

Every Child Ready to Read @ Your Library
www.pla.org/earlyliteracy.htm

Hennepin County Library (MN): Birth to Six
www.hclib.org/BirthTo6/

Mother Goose Society
www.librarysupport.net/mothergoosesociety/

Multnomah County (OR) Public Library: Early Words
www.multcolib.org/birthtosix/

National Association of Education for the Young Child
www.naeyc.org/

Nursery Rhymes at the Virtual Vine
www.thevirtualvine.com/nurseryrhymes.html

Project ECLIPSE: Mother Goose
eclipse.rutgers.edu/goose/literacy/

Public Library of Charlotte & Mecklenburg County: Grow & Learn @ Your Library
www.plcmc.org/forKids/growlearn/

Reading Is Fundamental (RIF)
www.rif.org

A Rhyme a Week: Nursery Rhymes for Early Literacy
curry.edschool.virginia.edu/go/wil/rimes_and_rhymes.htm

West Bloomfield Township Public Library (MI): Grow Up Reading @ the West Bloomfield Township Public Library
www.growupreading.org

Zero to Three's Brain Wonders
www.zerotothree.org/brainwonders/